PSYCHOTHERAPY

THORSONS
PRINCIPLES
OF

PSYCHOTHERAPY

BRICE AVERY

Thorsons
An Imprint of HarperCollins*Publishers*

Thorsons
An Imprint of HarperCollins*Publishers*
77–85 Fulham Palace Road
Hammersmith, London W6 8JB
1160 Battery Street
San Francisco, California 94111–1213

Published by Thorsons 1996
3 5 7 9 10 8 6 4

A catalogue record for this book
is available from the British Library

ISBN 0 7225 3348 9

Printed and bound in Great Britain by
Caledonian International Book Manufacturing Ltd, Glasgow

THIS BOOK IS DEDICATED TO PETER GOOZEE
FOR WHOM, TO THE GREAT RELIEF OF THOSE WHO
LOVE HIM, NO AMOUNT OF PSYCHOTHERAPY
WOULD MAKE THE SLIGHTEST DIFFERENCE

CONTENTS

INTRODUCING PSYCHOTHERAPY

HOW TO USE THIS BOOK

This book is intended both as a description of the various psychotherapies and as a guide to them. In describing each one I have stuck to the same basic structure so that the reader can easily compare the theories, techniques and antecedents of each one. However, I will begin this introduction with a brief description of the history of psychotherapy. The idea behind this is very much the same as the idea behind learning the history of a country before visiting it: things make more sense when you know the forces that have shaped them.

Having digested the history of a country, the sensible traveller tries to grasp some of the language of the place. Putting words to feelings and symptoms will help the reader to work out what they are looking for in a therapy, as they compare their needs with the strengths and weaknesses of each approach.

And so to the various cities and regions of the country that is modern psychotherapy. The eleven psychotherapies that are dealt with in depth have been chosen because they are the eleven most common therapies available that also fulfil the descriptive criteria on page 7. Those that are dealt with more briefly may be just as creditable but simply less widespread.

When considering psychotherapy, one of the hardest things to do is to make contact with an organization offering therapy, or with an individual psychotherapist. This is where Chapter Four: **Getting Started** is designed to be of service. If the reader is well informed and has thought through some of their personal issues before lifting the phone, the whole process of getting into the right therapy with the right therapist will be as smooth as possible.

My aim throughout has been to write an introduction to psychotherapy that bridges the gap between the first thoughts someone may have about needing some psychotherapy and the first phone call they make to actually start the process. I hope I have succeeded.

A BRIEF HISTORY OF PSYCHOTHERAPY

This brief history is designed to be read with reference to the chart opposite. Readers may find it difficult to see how everything fits together at this early stage but reference to the detailed descriptions which follow in Chapter Two will make things clearer.

For as long as mankind has existed, interpersonal psychology has been an important part of the healing of one person by another. Holy men, witch doctors, faith healers and the like probably all relied on some kind of empathy with their patients to effect a cure, or the illusion of a cure. Even western medicine has, especially in the past, leant heavily upon the mystique of the practitioners and the faith of the patients for part of its curative effect.

By the middle of the nineteenth century, and well into the twentieth, a lecture from their doctor was the only kind of psychotherapy that the emotionally troubled individual, who was not considered insane, could expect. Depending upon the

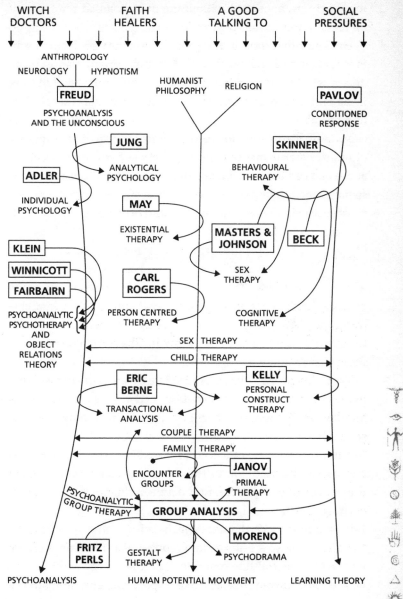

WITCH DOCTORS · FAITH HEALERS · A GOOD TALKING TO · SOCIAL PRESSURES

ANTHROPOLOGY

NEUROLOGY · HYPNOTISM

HUMANIST PHILOSOPHY · RELIGION

FREUD · **PAVLOV**

PSYCHOANALYSIS AND THE UNCONSCIOUS · CONDITIONED RESPONSE

JUNG · **SKINNER**

ANALYTICAL PSYCHOLOGY · BEHAVIOURAL THERAPY

ADLER · **MAY**

INDIVIDUAL PSYCHOLOGY · EXISTENTIAL THERAPY · **MASTERS & JOHNSON** · **BECK**

KLEIN · **WINNICOTT** · **FAIRBAIRN** · **CARL ROGERS** · SEX THERAPY

PSYCHOANALYTIC PSYCHOTHERAPY AND OBJECT RELATIONS THEORY · PERSON CENTRED THERAPY · COGNITIVE THERAPY

SEX | THERAPY

CHILD | THERAPY

ERIC BERNE · **KELLY**

PERSONAL CONSTRUCT THERAPY

TRANSACTIONAL ANALYSIS

COUPLE | THERAPY

FAMILY | THERAPY

ENCOUNTER GROUPS · **JANOV**

PRIMAL THERAPY

PSYCHOANALYTIC GROUP THERAPY · **GROUP ANALYSIS**

MORENO

FRITZ PERLS · GESTALT THERAPY · PSYCHODRAMA

PSYCHOANALYSIS · HUMAN POTENTIAL MOVEMENT · LEARNING THEORY

temperament of the doctor concerned, this would either be in the form of sympathetic encouragement or an admonishment for foolishness.

The story that then develops is of the right person being in the right place at the right time. Sigmund Freud was a young doctor who specialized in neurology. He was interested in hypnosis and was widely read in philosophy and anthropology. Living in Vienna, in Central Europe, he was well placed to get caught up in the explosion of philosophical and scientific thought, experimentation and application that was taking place at the end of the nineteenth century. Demonstrations of hypnosis happened to be popular at the time and Freud noticed that some of the invisible, although apparently real to the subject, physical maladies that hypnosis could induce — such as loss of the use of a limb, or 'forgetting' something that they had long known – were similar to those he had noticed in so-called 'hysterical' patients. He began to wonder if hidden forces of the psyche were at work in creating these symptoms. By asking this question and looking for the answer, Freud brought into the forefront of modern thinking the idea that much of who and what we are, and what drives and motivates us, is hidden from our everyday awareness. Thus began an exploration that mapped out our unconscious, described *defence mechanisms*, as Freud provided the first model for the understanding and subsequent treatment of neurosis.

Initially Carl Jung followed Freud's ideas but over time his emphasis shifted towards the interpretation of fantasy and dream through a collaboration between therapist and patient; as Jung developed his independent theories of **Analytical Psychology** he drifted apart from Freud.

Adler was also a follower of Freud until 1910. Ultimately, he rejected the central Freudian idea that the energy driving us is derived from a primitive, hedonistic pool of desire called the *id*.

Instead, Adler emphasized the social factors in human development. His theory, called **Individual Psychology**, is preoccupied with how the patient's lifestyle has developed. Unlike Freud, Adler's theories are not widely used. Nevertheless, they undoubtedly contributed to the many other therapies that later developed, partly inspired by Freud and partly by the more accessible social and educational paradigms which began to spring up, especially in the USA, later in the century.

Later, three people in particular – Melanie Klein, D. W. Winnicott and Fairbairn (*see* **Psychoanalytic Psychotherapy**) – contributed to what became the British School, based on the elaboration, modification, and extension of Freud's ideas. Their theories place emphasis upon the relations between individuals and rely upon an understanding of the way key relationships are represented inside the person. Thus the basic drive is neither instinctual or purely social, but based upon a desire to relate to others: to love and be loved in return.

As the century progressed, and largely after the Second World War, new therapies emerged which were far more accessible and easily grasped by an increasingly interested public. Each of these therapies was distinguished by holding a different set of basic assumptions about the nature of man's psyche. Carl Rogers developed **Person Centred Therapy**, or **PCT**, which holds that everyone is whole and good and well-motivated at the core of their beings and that the task of therapy is to draw this out. More than any other therapy, **PCT** is what is meant by the term 'counselling', although the word 'counselling' is now so blurred and overused that it is best avoided in the interests of clarity.

Transactional Analysis, or **TA**, whilst growing up in the same rich soil of the so-called 'Human Potential Movement', (a sort of umbrella term for therapies and theories which aim to be accessible and useful to as many people as possible) owed much to

6   Freud's original ideas. For example, the mental apparatus postulated by Freud of *id*, *ego* and *superego* is reflected in the **TA** ego states of, respectively, *child*, *adult* and *parent*. Another important aspect of **TA** is the fact that it takes place in groups.

The earliest truly psychotherapeutic work with groups began in a very small but significant way, early in the century, in the army. Here it was used to help those suffering from war neurosis. This grew into **Group Analysis**: that form of group work which uses psychoanalytic, or Freudian, ideas for its rationale. Apart from **TA**, the main interactions between group working and the 'Human Potential Movement' are **Gestalt Therapy**, **Primal Therapy**, **Psychodrama** and **Encounter**.

All these therapies, however, take a particular stance in relation to Freud's work. This is because the instigators of new therapies have often experienced analysis and subsequently turned away from its precepts; for example, Fritz Perls (of **Gestalt**) and Arthur Janov (of **Primal Therapy**). Or if they have not experienced therapy they nonetheless struggle to get out from under Freud's shadow. An example is J. L. Moreno who founded **Psychodrama** and who was always insistent that this was better than psychoanalysis, and that he was superior to Freud – but if Moreno did not feel himself to be under Freud's shadow then why was he preoccupied with triumphing over him?

The third main strand is that of the 'Learning Theories', such as **Behavioural Psychology** which was developed by Skinner and others – principally in North America. **Behavioural Therapy** is probably the psychotherapy that is most distant in its basic assumptions from those that have developed from Freud's ideas. With their emphasis on observable behaviour and objective assessment, **Behavioural** and related **Cognitive Therapies** are immensely practical. These pioneers and therapies, along with all the therapies mentioned in the chart, are explained in greater detail in Chapters Two and Three.

Many other therapies have developed in the conceptual space between the 'Human Potential Movement' and 'Learning Theory': **Rational Emotive Therapy**, **Couple Therapy**, **Bereavement Counselling**, **Sex Therapy** and **Behavioural Modification Groups**. The attraction and value of these therapies is the way in which they are geared to achieving goals and are limited in time, and can be used to focus on specific problems.

By referring to the diagram, readers will see the relations between the various therapies I have just briefly described demonstrated schematically. To some there may be unexpected absences. Two obvious examples are **Hypnotherapy** and **Neuro-Linguistic Programming** (which has hypno-therapeutic elements). This illustrates a particular problem, namely that the boundaries designating what is and what is not psychotherapy are not clear. For this reason I have used somewhat arbitrary, but I hope sensible, criteria to limit the scope of this guide whilst at the same time dealing reasonably comprehensively with the subject. These criteria are:

> Does the therapy have a forcefully convincing theory of the human psyche that informs the therapy?
>
> Is the therapy an active, rather than passive, process for both the patient and the therapist?
>
> Is it in current widespread usage?
>
> Is the therapy based primarily on the imaginative use of language? In other words, is it a 'talking cure'?
>
> Does it involve a relationship between at least two people in its practice?

As well as fulfilling these criteria, each of the therapies described places at least some emphasis on all or most of the following general assumptions of relational psychotherapy:

That the relationship between the patient and therapist will be important to the process of the therapy.

That a greater choice of thought, action and emotion is possible for the individual involved as a result of therapy.

That the action of the therapy will reveal aspects of thought, action and emotion to the patient that they were previously unaware of.

That the therapeutic relationship will make it possible for the patient to confront and examine difficult or upsetting realities about themselves.

That there is a desire and ability on the part of the patient to learn from the therapeutic process and to develop the capacity to work through difficulties in an increasingly independent manner.

This then is our starting point. In the next section we shall examine some of the ideas, feelings and emotions that prompt people towards seeking psychotherapy.

PUTTING WORDS TO FEELINGS

The previous chapter gave a sense of where the psychotherapies came from. Now, before moving on to discuss the main therapies in detail, it is worth looking closely at some of the most common and appropriate reasons for seeking therapy. With this information in mind, the reader will be better equipped to understand the ways in which the various psychotherapies respond to the needs of their patients; or, as some therapists prefer to say, clients.

One of the most troubling realizations to make is that things go wrong in our relationships over and over again in the same way. Freud put it very well:

> We have come across people all of whose human relationships have the same outcome: such as the benefactor who is abandoned in anger after a time by each of his *protégés*, how ever much they may otherwise differ from one another, and who thus seems doomed to taste all the bitterness of ingratitude; or the man whose friendships all end in betrayal by his friend; or the man who time after time in the course of his life raises someone else to a position of great private or public authority and replaces him by a new one; or, again, the lover each of whose love affairs with a woman passes through the same phases and reaches the same conclusion.

Having once caught a glimpse of this tendency in oneself it is impossible to forget it. Attempts to resolve it for oneself are rarely successful, partly because 'solving things for oneself' is likely to be part of the problem. Also, because there is always more to the story than we are consciously aware of and this cannot be brought into view from the unconscious without someone else's help. Invariably, the compulsion to go on repeating behaviour in relationships that harms our wellbeing or that of someone else comes from our past. Unconsciously, we re-enact the disturbed relationships of our childhood and unwittingly pick out individuals from around us who will – for similar reasons of their own – be compelled to join in.

THE UNBEARABLE FEELING OF BEING 'STUCK'

Sometimes the feeling or sensation that prompts someone to seek psychotherapy is the mental equivalent of wading through treacle and coming to a halt in front of an invisible barrier. Exhausted, undermined and very low in spirits, some people resign themselves to their plight and try to lessen the pain by convincing themselves that this is all there is in life, that this is all they can expect and that they probably deserve everything anyway. Others seek help with what hope they have left.

A GENERAL DISSATISFACTION WITH LIFE

This is related to, but different from, the feeling of being stuck. General dissatisfaction is a sort of creeping malaise that slowly infiltrates an individual's life and makes the future seem predictable and unexciting. The courage to recognize this state of affairs and wish to move on in some way can drive individuals to extraordinary lengths. For instance, some people sell up and start a new life, others separate from long-term partners and still others buy boats and sail around the world. These 'environmental modifications' seldom work because the inner emotional world of the individual stays the same. There is something of the truth of this in the well-known Oriental saying: 'No matter how far a man sails, his horizon stays the same'.

The courageous thing to do when generally dissatisfied with life is to find out where the dissatisfaction comes from through some form of introspection. Many people are afraid that this will make them feel worse, and initially this might happen. However, this fear should be compared with the sinking feeling you may have in a few years' time, when a massive change or upheaval in your life has made no real difference.

Sometimes a life crisis overwhelms an individual's capacity to cope with emotional issues that may have always bothered them, but which have previously not been debilitating. The three types of crisis are:

Relational – such as abandonment by a partner, bereavement, or changing relations with a parent or child.

Personal – such as the discovery of a serious disease, for example AIDS or Cancer.

Environmental – such as the loss of your house or your job, having an unexpected child, even sudden wealth.

BEING HAUNTED BY THE PAST

Like Swift's Gulliver, pinned down by hundreds of tiny threads, individuals often come to realize that they are restricted in the present by a myriad of remembered incidents from, and attitudes towards, their past. The principal source of the frustration is the sensation that nothing can be fully enjoyed or entered into – there is always a knot in the stomach or a dread at the back of the mind that cannot quite be forgotten. For many people there are also strong grievances towards individuals who they feel have let them down. In time, grievances – especially those that can never actually be put right by the perpetrator – become like a shrine to be constantly returned to and worshipped at. A person in this position may unwittingly spend their lives wrecking their relationships because they are both looking for someone to take away the hurt that was done (which is impossible) or to pay for the hurt that was done (which is also impossible).

DEPRESSION

Depression is a common problem that runs on a continuum. At one end there are the sort of feelings that go with things going wrong or with a loss of direction in life; in the middle is a debilitating loss of ability to cope with everyday life because of, for example, severe anxiety, or worry following loss, or a life crisis; at the other end of the spectrum is full-blown clinical depression. Depression in the worse half of the continuum is characterized by difficulty sleeping, loss of appetite, feelings of hopelessness, low energy, loss of sexual interest and an inability to concentrate. Some of the psychotherapies are good at helping with the psychological aspects of depression. The more severe depressive states are caused by chemical imbalances in the brain and will need medication from a psychiatrist or family practitioner. If you are in any doubt about the basis of depressive or even suicidal feelings you should always consult a doctor before starting any psychotherapy.

ANXIETY

Anxiety is a common symptom of everyday life and probably originates in our very important and primitive capacity to be afraid. In the psychological setting, anxiety is often troubling because it seems to have no cause. In reality, the cause is hidden from our awareness in our unconscious – that part of our psychological functioning of which we are unaware. Hidden or forbidden impulses, thoughts or attitudes cause anxiety when they threaten to surface into awareness. Our usual reaction to anxiety, almost before we are aware of it, is to push the unwanted feelings – such as anger or sexual desire – back down again with a suitable defence. Defences are discussed in Chapter Two under **Psychoanalysis**.

When anxiety can no longer be satisfactorily controlled it surfaces as one of the usual symptoms that bring people to therapy:

There are many different kinds of phobia, some better known than others. Whether the fear is of other people, spiders, exams or dirt, anxiety is one of the chief symptoms associated with the phobia. Behavioural therapies seek to minimize the anxiety and hence reduce the power of the phobic object or situation. Alternatively, psychotherapies such as **Psychoanalysis** take the view that the phobia is an outward expression of a repressed conflict and that the conflict needs to be investigated and understood so that the overt behaviour is no longer 'needed'.

RELATIONAL DIFFICULTIES

Many relational difficulties become more pressing at certain times of life, such as when children become more independent, when middle age is reached, or when retirement (early or otherwise) is considered.

Common examples are:

Relations between women and their mothers.

Relations between men and their fathers (especially when the fathers die).

Relations between married couples.

PROBLEMS IN GROUPS

Many people find group situations difficult. To an extent this is only to be expected, as socialization is the most complex human activity. Nevertheless there are those for whom groups hold particular terror. Usually such individuals have had deprived or distorted experiences in their first life group, the family. By persistently avoiding situations that they expect will be, or that begin to feel, similar to those that made them anxious and confused when young, they become isolated adults. An example of

this would be someone whose family could not disagree without rage, rejection and verbal cruelty. As adults, this person consequently avoids negotiation, confrontation and management of strong opinions in their relationships. Paradoxically such people often end up with managerial type posts because although they work hard to belong to a group, they do it in a way that (they hope) avoids confrontation because they are in charge. Autocratic fathers, head teachers and politicians, as well as managers, are examples of people trying to belong without properly being part of the group process. For some people social isolation is a workable option, but for most holding down a job and having a family requires some level of confidence in group situations.

WORK RELATIONS

Stress in the work place is one of the most common difficulties experienced by people who are otherwise content. Whatever the apparent cause, poor relations between people is the main cause of unhappiness at work. On the large scale this involves industrial relations and institutional dynamics. As far as individuals are concerned, the best way to tackle stress at work is for the individual to understand their own part in causing it, work out what they can change and what they can not, and accommodate accordingly, using their new knowledge as a defence against despair and frustration. If this is not possible a new and better position will probably be sought. In this case, however, at least this big decision will have been preceded by an increased personal awareness and, which, as I have discussed earlier, is the only sensible way to make such changes.

An individual's motivation for seeking psychotherapy is rarely as straightforward as just wanting to find out more; nevertheless this is often part of the motivation. Human beings are naturally curious, and generally inclined towards those things that are at the same time exciting and bring a feeling of wellbeing. Many psychotherapeutic encounters offer both of these aspects, and are thus an attractive process in which to become involved. However there are two particular problems that stem from this. Firstly, there is a tendency for those therapies that are sensational, dramatic or particularly emotional to mistake 'an experience' for increased awareness and expansion of personal choice. Secondly, those individuals prone to become 'growthaholics' find they can not manage without being in some sort of psychotherapy. Not only does this sometimes make it hard for them to move on emotionally, it also makes them prey to unscrupulous or ignorant therapists.

WANTING TO BE A THERAPIST

Some people know that they want to be a therapist and recognize that having therapy is the best start. Others do not realize that they want to be therapists and can unwittingly sabotage their own therapeutic experience by competing with the therapist.

SPECIFIC REASONS FOR SEEKING THERAPY

There are a host of specific reasons for seeking therapy many of which have agencies or groups dedicated to them. A brief list is given below, but for further details readers are referred to the list of *Frequently Asked Questions* in Chapter Four at the end of the book.

Some reasons for seeking therapy:

Eating disorders (such as bulimia, anorexia, obesity)

Child sex abuse

Abortion

AIDS

Alcoholism

Substance abuse

Bereavement

Phobias

Rape

THE MAIN PSYCHOTHERAPIES

PSYCHOANALYSIS

BACKGROUND

Towards the end of the nineteenth century, Sigmund Freud (1856-1939), an Austrian doctor of medicine and neurology, began to develop a series of ideas about human psychological functioning. These not only became **Psychoanalysis** but also came to form the roots of many other more recent therapies.

Partly because Psychoanalysis has been around for so long and partly because it is as much a set of ideas as a curative technique, there are many minor variations practised on the original theme. There is however a core consensus on the theory and practise of Psychoanalysis which we shall consider next.

THE PSYCHOANALYTIC VIEW OF THE PERSON

Central to Psychoanalysis is the *unconscious*. This is best thought of as by far the largest part of the psyche. Indeed, the unconscious is much larger than the part that we are aware of, the conscious part, and the parts that can be brought to awareness with a struggle – the *preconscious*. Ideas, impulses and desires are banished to the realm of the unconscious because if they enter, or threaten to enter the conscious life, they produce uncomfortable levels of anxiety or even terror.

At this point a brief description of the *id*, *ego* and *superego*, or what Freud termed the 'Mental Apparatus', is necessary:

The *id* is the animal heart of the person. It is the source of instinctual desire and impulse. Having no need for external influences because it is its own source of energy, it exists for the instantaneous gratification of itself. Every animal has some sort of id and Freud considered the human id as the fountainhead of all human motivation. It is present from birth, perhaps even from conception.

The *ego* is the part of the mental apparatus responsible for managing reality. In practical terms this means the area that deals with relationships with other people, as well as the emotional life of the individual. In fulfilling its function, the ego attempts to meet the needs of the id, whilst avoiding situations that are life threatening or intolerably anxiety-provoking. Because of this the ego is often in the position of suppressing the desires of the id, if these are not in the interests of the whole person (that is, the id, ego and superego).

The *superego* develops as the person interacts with their emotional surroundings – usually their parents – and is perhaps best thought of as forming the conscience. The superego rewards and punishes the ego for its ability to avoid anxiety-provoking material surfacing from the unconscious, whilst at the same time it – the ego – struggles to meet the needs of the id.

The reader will appreciate that the id and the superego are inevitably in conflict. If the ego cannot find a compromise then the conflict will be consigned to the unconscious.

When something is consigned to the unconscious it does not disappear – rather, it finds altered or disguised forms of expressing itself. Usually this is through the *defence mechanisms* by which an unwanted thought, impulse or desire is apparently banished, but surfaces in some other way. Defence mechanisms have their own often destructive and limiting consequences in everyday life. Here are some of the common defence mechanisms:

Repression – Upsetting things are simply forgotten. This could be something from childhood which would make life intolerable, such as sexual longing for a parent, or something more recent like an appointment at the dentist.

Denial – A block is placed against a particular facet of reality so that it seems not to exist. Someone terrified of cancer might deny the existence of a lump, or someone afraid of their destructive impulses might be unable to see that they get angry and abusive in certain situations.

Projection – An attitude or desire that one finds disturbing in oneself is transferred or put into someone else. Many people who are quick to call others racist or sexist are unable to face these tendencies in themselves.

Displacement – An impulse or desire that is unacceptable because of who it is aimed at, such as rage towards an overbearing father, might be displaced onto other authority figures such as the police or a boss at work.

Reaction Formation – This is the generation of powerful attitudes or desires that are the opposite of those which are really held. Someone troubled by homosexual tendencies

may be vehemently anti-homosexual (as distinct from homophobic which is a normal heterosexual reaction under certain circumstances).

Rationalization – Here, troubling activities or desires are legitimized by recourse to shaky moral or rational high ground: 'She was asking for it', or 'It's not really stealing because everyone does it', are examples of rationalization. Cruelty often becomes rationalized into 'parental duty' by parents as a defence against their sadistic impulses towards the child.

Reversal – This is a little like displacement. Impulses which are believed, accurately or not, to lead to unacceptable consequences are turned in upon oneself. Most self-destructive urges can be found to be reversals of aggression towards unacceptable targets. Self-mutilating teenagers, for instance, may be enraged with someone else but have despaired of being able to express their rage without intolerable repercussions. The worst repercussion is, of course, to be ignored or misunderstood.

Introjection – This is when a person ingests and makes part of their own psyche that which is someone else's. This is often the result of someone else's projection and is one of the most powerful mechanisms by which overbearing *super-egos* are created in the child.

THE LINK BETWEEN PAST AND PRESENT

All the above *defence mechanisms* are used by the developing infant in the face of external influences upon the desires of the *id*. In the child the id is in the ascendant: the child is the centre of its own universe, all desires are immediate and represent all parts of the physical and emotional person. Such an idyll cannot last and, as we have seen, the *ego* develops to try and manage the clash between the demands of the id and the expectations of the external emotional world. Thus the ego uses defence mechanisms to banish those conflicts it can not resolve.

Freud believed that the *id/ego/superego* relationships that develop in childhood are carried forward into adulthood. He called this the *compulsion to repeat*, although these compulsions are best understood as an inevitable result of any of the defence mechanisms listed above. For example, a child may grow up in a family where the natural rage the child feels when it is disappointed is taken by the parent as an attack on the parent's ability. Such a child will, in all likelihood, be shamed and admonished for its angry outbursts. But the child's rage in the face of its frustration does not magically go away. Instead this rage is repressed, because it threatens the child's closeness to its parent and is therefore terrifying. The child grows up frightened of its own capacity for rage and anger because it never has the chance to express it and so regulate it of its own accord. As an adult, such a person will be unable to face realities within themselves and between themselves and others, especially where there is real anger or frustration around. Such a person will have great difficulty in forming well-rounded relationships. Added to this, such a person will occasionally explode with rage for an apparently trivial reason as the repressed frustration becomes too much for the ego. The effect of this is to bring in criticism from the superego, and the resulting shame which rains down on the ego thus confirms the apparent need for further repression.

Of course, when such a person has a child they will inflict the same injunctions on their child's developing ego, and this child will grow up to perpetuate the problem. (Unless they can recognize the problem first, and do something about it!)

The patient, referred to as the *analysand*, and the analyst meet five times a week for fifty minutes. The analysand lies on a couch so that the analyst is not visible. The analysand is then encouraged to say whatever comes into their mind – which is, in fact, only possible if there are no defences at work. Lying quiescent with few distractions, the patient finds him or herself on the brink of their unconscious, where to say whatever comes to mind is to risk links being made between ideas and memories in such a way that repressed material and desires begin to take shadowy form on the edge of their awareness.

In nearly every case, the analysand will resist this process in all the ways they have throughout their life, but in this instance it will be in the presence of an analyst.

The analyst has a set of tasks to perform that sound simple, but are actually extremely difficult:

Neutrality – this is the important ability to neither suppress nor gratify the emerging unconscious desires. To do either, to excess, will stop or slow down the process.

Confrontation – the analyst, by considering what it is like to be with the patient, reflects back what is going on. For instance, the analyst may say to the patient: 'You are telling me how helpful coming here is but I think you might actually fear that it is of no use.'

Interpretation – this is an attempt by the analyst to throw light on the patient's behaviour in a way that is new to the patient, for example: 'Perhaps being positive about coming here is because you fear that I will lose interest in you, like your father did, if you don't do well.' (*For a further elaboration of the use of interpretation see Psychoanalytic Psychotherapy*).

Reconstruction – This is where the analyst reconstructs something from the past with added meaning for the present, thus: 'Perhaps you don't want to hear the things I have to say, even if they are helpful, because I sound like your father giving you a lecture.'

Use of these techniques helps repressed material emerge into awareness between the analyst and analysand so that another crucial process can occur. The analysand progressively mistakes the analyst for significant others in their past; the analyst, by accepting this process, helps re-create the early emotional scene of the child. This so-called *transference neurosis* becomes the heart of the analysis as the analytic couple work through the reasons for the defences and resistance.

The aim of Psychoanalysis is simply to increase insight so that aspects of the unconscious are made conscious. Thus the patient (or analysand) is equipped with self-knowledge and consequently is given the opportunity to choose what he or she does and how they do it.

CRITICAL SUMMARY

Setting – At a therapy centre or in the consulting rooms of the analyst. Patients invariably lie on a couch, with the analyst sitting in a chair behind their head and out of view.

Aim – To bring to consciousness that which is repressed in the unconscious so that the patient is freer to have mutual relationships with others that are firmly grounded in reality, rather than constantly repeating their past conflicts.

Technique – By working regularly and over a long time use is made of free association, dreams, and the relationship that the patient attempts to have with the therapist.

24 **Good points** – Psychoanalysis is one of the therapies capable of working its way to the bedrock of the person's disturbed development, and hence to the basis of some of the most debilitating problems in life.

Often effective for – The compulsion to repeat, problems from the past, anxiety problems, phobias, and problems relating to others.

Bad points – Some practitioners are rather rigid adherents to the letter of psychoanalytic technique and can be found to be rather remote and unsupportive within the therapeutic relationship.

Seldom effective for – Crisis intervention, alcoholism or addiction.

Cost – Generally high. Occasionally there are arrangements made between training organizations and the NHS which make provision for psychoanalysis for minimal fees (*contact the British Psychoanalytic Society, see Resource Guide*).

Availability – Widespread, but tends to be confined to urban areas.

Commitment – High; attendance is usually five times a week for several years.

Training – Intensive and long. All analysts must undergo their own analysis.

BACKGROUND

We come now to a difficult though very important task. Despite its rather cumbersome and possibly off-putting name, **Psychoanalytic Psychotherapy**, in all its various guises, is one of the most practised and effective psychotherapies available. Psychoanalytic Psychotherapy is a direct derivative of Freudian analysis, with important modifications, additions and subtractions in both the theory and the practice. In practice it can take place as infrequently as once a week or, like classical psychoanalysis, five times a week. Sessions are invariably fifty minutes long and patients may lie on the couch using the techniques of *free association*, or sit in armchairs and deliberately focus on a problem. Psychoanalytic Psychotherapy differs from *counselling* in that it uses the ideas of Freud, and often those of Klein, Fairbairn and Winnicott (as I shall discuss below), rather than those stemming directly from the humanist movement and Carl Rogers. Nevertheless, such is the protean nature of psychotherapy that there are many counsellors trained in the theories of psychoanalytic psychotherapy who practise what is known as **Psychodynamic Counselling**.

HOW PSYCHOANALYTIC PSYCHOTHERAPY VIEWS THE PERSON

This is a concise description of Psychoanalytic Psychotherapy and, as with the other therapies described, I can only give a flavour of the attitude this therapy adopts towards the individual and their psyche. The contributions to Psychoanalytic Psychotherapy come from three innovative and representative therapists who placed their ideas and experience within the broad context of Freudian practice. They represent a view slightly different, though many believe not incompatible with,

that of Freud, in the matter of human psychological development. These therapists were interested in the deepest levels of our development and sought to understand how our course is altered or disrupted by the vicissitudes of early life. These three representative therapists are Melanie Klein, R. D. Fairbairn and D. W. Winnicott.

MELANIE KLEIN (1882–1960)

Although she worked within the broad psychoanalytic fold, Melanie Klein developed a theory of personality development that states that the basic motivation of the individual is not first and foremost towards pleasure (a Freudian concept), but towards other people – initially mother, then the wider world. The desire of the infant is to relate to others. In the Kleinian view this simple-sounding process is complicated by the innate ambivalence that the infant feels towards others (also known as *objects*). The successful negotiation within the infant of both loving and hating the breast, then all of mother, and so on to other people and all relationships, is problematic. After extensive observation and psychoanalysis of small children, Klein formed the belief that infants both envy the breast/mother/others because they have good things they want, but also use it/them as a dumping ground for feelings and ideas that seem incompatible with desire, such as hate and murderousness. The infant psyche is thus left split in what Klein called the *paranoid-schizoid position*: accepting desire of others requires denial of hate; acknowledging hatred requires repression of desire.

Underdeveloped adults are those that persist in this split. They cannot tolerate the capacity for the simultaneous existence of both hate and love, either in themselves or in others. They will see others as all good or all bad, and themselves likewise. Their friendships will be like those of the school playground. Successfully developed adults have discovered and worked through the painful truth that the breast/mother/other that they hate is the same breast/mother/other as the one they love. This is called the *depressive position* and it is healthy because it is founded in reality: relations are seen as being made up of hate and love, creativity and destruction, giving and taking, and they are tolerated as such. Most people are a mixture of paranoid-schizoid and depressive positions when they come for therapy. Therapy from a Kleinian point of view is aimed at helping the patient from the paranoid-schizoid to the depressive position.

R. D. FAIRBAIRN (1889–1964)

R. D. Fairbairn made contributions in the area of the *ego* – that part of the self which is balanced between the primitive desires of the *id* and the demands of the *superego*. (*See Psychoanalysis*). He proposed that whereas in Freudian theory the ego had been developed for impulse control and adaptation to the demands of reality, it could in fact usefully be thought of as the core of the person. Fairbairn considered that the child is born with a pristine and complete ego which becomes split, altered and selectively repressed as it passes through the vicissitudes of relating to others, or *objects*. This process starts with the mother and moves on to other people. From a Fairbairnian point of view, therapy is aimed at reacquainting these split parts with one another.

D. W. WINNICOTT (1896–1971)

D. W. Winnicott did not propound theories in quite the same way as Klein and Fairbairn. Instead, he contributed many ideas and different ways of looking at the developing psyche, and a particular attitude to patients. Probably because he was a paediatrician as well as a psychoanalyst, the mother and child had a central place in his thinking. He made many contributions to the way that the mother and child relate to one another, described in terms of what had by then become known as *object relations*: the way in which the baby relates to others and comes to terms with the fact that it is not the centre of the universe.

One of the ways this happens is through what Winnicott described as *good enough mothering*. This notion embodies the idea that a good mother is one who is capable of occasionally letting the child down, both in action and temperament, as time progresses. Thus the mother gently encourages appropriate levels of independence to coexist along with the dependency of childhood. In this way the child increasingly senses its individuality in a realistic way, and builds good object relations. Disruption in the gradual process of learning to *object-relate* results, according to Winnicott, in the creation of a 'false self' which acts as a screen to protect the 'true self' of the individual. An example of the effect this might have in the adult would be the person who becomes, paradoxically, more withdrawn and incapable of being helped the closer a friend, lover or therapist tries to draw towards them: the true self begins to respond but is so afraid of being hurt or let down again that it cannot help but activate the defensive false self. A Psychoanalytic Psychotherapist who is influenced by Winnicott will work to survive the attacks by the false self in the expectation that the true self will in time reveal itself for emotional attachment.

HOW PSYCHOANALYTIC
PSYCHOTHERAPY HELPS

A typical Psychoanalytic Psychotherapist will work with fundamental ideas from Freud, as well as the valuable refinements made by contributors such as those mentioned above. Whatever the emphasis, the aim is that the patient should learn to surrender themselves to the process so that the relationship – even though it is strange in that it does not involve direct input from the therapist's own life – can develop, and be studied minutely by the pair as they try to work together. The assumption is that the way the patient attempts to relate to the therapist mirrors the way that they try to relate elsewhere. The crucial differences are that within this relationship the usual social collusion that people go along with in order to interact without embarrassment is dropped, and the reason the relationship exists in the first place is to uncover the true nature of the patient.

In practical terms many techniques are used:

Free Association – This is Freud's fundamental rule that the patient should try to say whatever comes into their head without editing or organizing their thoughts. This is much harder than it sounds because material that feels upsetting or even potentially offensive to the therapist or patient may be repressed. Wrestling with these difficulties reveals much about the inner conflicts that the individual has concerning themselves and their relations with others.

Clarification – The therapist takes nothing for granted and avoids assuming that they know what the patient means by a throwaway remark. In this way, hidden thoughts and attitudes are brought into the light of day.

Linking – The therapist tries to make links between aspects of what the patient says and does, and their behaviour, either in the sessions or from the past. The aim is to shed new light upon the way the patient trips themselves up by re-enacting repressed childhood conflicts.

Interpretation – Another key technique taken from Psychoanalysis, this involves attempts by the therapist to make unconscious motives, attitudes and feelings conscious, in order that the patient's personal insight is increased.

Everything is potentially open to interpretation: comments, fantasies, dreams, lateness, avoiding painful issues, attitudes to the therapist and so on. Specific and important areas for interpretation that are also common in psychoanalysis are the links between early life, conflicts within the psyche, and behaviour in the session.

The four main kinds of interpretation are:

Transference – Transference feelings are those feelings the patient has towards the therapist when they mistake the therapist for some significant person, or *object*, in their past. These feelings are encouraged, or at least not stopped, because interpreting them reveals so much about what is going on emotionally inside the patient.

Defences – Defence mechanisms (*see Psychoanalysis*) include projecting one's own feelings onto others, denying reality, intellectualizing and rationalizing away the real and sometimes uncomfortable basis of behaviours and attitudes. These mechanisms cannot be interrupted until they are interpreted.

Conscience – Burdensome guilt has to be traced to its source through the process of interpretation, so that an understanding can be reached as to the ways in which the patient has learnt to attack and sabotage him or her self from within. Often it is found that the attacked parts are those that feel dangerous or unwanted; in fact, often these parts contain the patient's ability for spontaneity and/or capacity to receive affection.

Confrontation – Occasionally it is necessary for interpretations to be 'buttressed' with direct confrontation. The therapist stands firm and gently insists upon the reality of some

Gradually, often over many sessions, the patient learns to take in the good and nourishing aspects of the interaction with the psychotherapist and so become more self-knowing, less at the mercy of archaic responses, and more capable of appropriate dependent and independent relations with others.

CRITICAL SUMMARY

Setting – Usually in a dedicated consulting room either at the home of the therapist or in an institute. This sort of Psychotherapy is available in a limited way within the NHS, so patients may be seen in the premises of local psychiatric or psychological services.

Aim – To bring to awareness the inner emotional world of the patient in order to improve their capacity to relate to others and to value themselves as they really are.

Technique – Some therapists use the couch whilst others face their patients. Sessions usually last for fifty minutes and may be once to four or five times a week. Most Psychoanalytic Psychotherapists have a particular emphasis, for example *psychoanalytic* or *object relations*, but a careful and rigorously thought out blend is used in day-to-day therapy.

Good points – This therapy is highly adaptable to various theoretical standpoints and therefore has a large, vibrant and thoughtful body of practitioners who interact creatively in journals and at conferences. The result is a continuously improved and considered body of theoretical and practical knowledge, thus a flexible and effective therapy is likely to be available to the patient.

Often effective for – Short and long-term therapy is available for those dissatisfied with life, who have had a traumatic past, who are depressed by their compulsion to repeat, who are unable to relate to others properly, or simply those interested in growing.

Bad points – Often intensive, usually quite expensive and only really suitable for those with time to spare, the inclination to think things over and a reasonable support network for the times when, inevitably, they feel rather disorientated.

Seldom effective for – This sort of therapy is not suitable for crisis intervention and is unlikely to be of much help to active alcoholics or other substance abusers.

Cost – Most Psychoanalytic Psychotherapy happens privately and can be quite a commitment. Nevertheless, everything is negotiable and most therapists are prepared to be flexible if a patient's income is low.

Availability – Widely available though seldom advertised. Most therapists are affiliated to larger organizations (*see Resource Guide*).

Commitment – This is often high; it depends upon the initial agreement with the therapist.

Training – As with Psychoanalysis, training is thorough and involves the therapist in their own analysis which may stretch over several years. As described above, there is a wide variety of theoretical standpoints represented in this broad school, which means that it is worth asking your possible future therapist what his or her training was. They should not mind telling you.

ANALYTICAL PSYCHOLOGY

BACKGROUND

Carl Jung (1875–1961) is almost as well known as Freud and for a time they had a mutually enriching relationship as fellow scientists and philosophers. However, even before they met, the younger man had already developed his own distinct view, to which he devoted himself when he and Freud quarrelled and parted company. Jung himself was averse to the idea of schools of thought and found the idea of followers and 'disciples' of his theories difficult to cope with. Freud was quite the opposite and this may have something to do with their apparently irreconcilable differences. Nevertheless Jungian therapy in one form or another has flourished, tending to appeal to those of a more artistic, or possibly romantic (in the classical sense of the term), disposition.

HOW ANALYTICAL PSYCHOLOGY VIEWS THE PERSON

Analytical Psychology believes a person is born containing a set of tools or templates called *archetypal structures*. These form complex reference points from which the external environment is explored and evaluated and the internal environment is judged for how adequate it is. The self, or *ego*, develops between these two as the infant *archetypes* unfold like butterfly wings and implicitly demand gratification. In the first instance these innate demands are for things like warmth, comfort, quietness and food. If the exploration of the external environment (in this instance the mother) is successful, then a close match develops between the archetype and the environment, with the ego consequently swelling in stature as it makes sense of the inner world of the whole person. As the ego becomes stronger and more resilient – through repeated, successful 'close matches'

between the templates of the archetypes and the realities of the external world – the child begins to be able to tolerate a degree of dissimilarity between the two.

This aspect of the Jungian view of the person is crucial because it explains why, despite the fact that everyone is born with the same *archetypal templates* – Jung called this the *collective unconscious* – we all grow up to be different from one another. As the ego develops it becomes capable of two important activities. Firstly, it can re-tune and weaken the archetypal expectations so as to create the individual's unique identity. Secondly, it can deal healthily with the many occasions on which external reality does not match the archetypal template. An example of this would be the way in which a healthy person grows from being a baby who becomes enraged when it is mildly frustrated (such as when it is not able to reach a toy or is not fed immediately) to a young adult with an ego which is able to recast *archetypal* rage (such as frustration with an uncooperative official) into assertive action within the external environment. Such activity further enhances the ego of the individual – though possibly not of the official!

THE ANALYTICAL PSYCHOLOGY EXPLANATION OF PSYCHOLOGICAL PROBLEMS

In this view, individuals at the healthy end of the spectrum will show the flexibility and robustness of their ego by creatively adapting to changes in the external environment, be they physical or emotional. Such an ego will also be one that, by definition, validates the individual's inner emotional world to create a strong sense of personal identity.

However, the ego feels persecuted when this process – of gradually accommodating the changing relationships between the individual's *archetypes* and their experience – is disrupted.

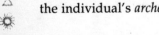

Under these circumstances, both the external environment and the inner world are less able to be sources of nourishment and developmental experience for the ego; instead they become sources of psychological disturbance. For example, if the 'external world', perhaps represented by a parent, repeatedly rejects a child's archetypal exploration or request for comfort, the child's ego becomes disturbed. It will be forced to pair up the part of itself that is aware of the need for comfort and cuddles with the primitive inborn 'instruction' to get comfort, and to force these to disappear, as it were locked together like two lovers, into the abyss of the *personal unconscious*. In Jungian terms the *personal unconscious* is distinguished from the *collective unconscious*, which can be thought of as a genetically inherited memory and potential for unconscious functioning and motivation. This is the wellspring of the archetypes.

Further disturbance of the individual can derive from an understimulating or depriving environment which ensures that a proportionately large area of personal potential remains unrealized. Under all these circumstances the internal environment becomes host to a deprived and understimulated ego.

Clearly, this state of affairs is very depressing to consider. Indeed, in Jungian terms, this is depression. Not unnaturally, the individual in this sort of situation will develop *maladaptive* strategies – analogous to *defences* – with which to escape the reality of their situation. Unfortunately, these very behaviours will ensure that the person's experience of the environment and their inner expectation of what is on offer will be at odds with each other and lead to disappointment. The only recourse is back to the maladaptive strategies and so the ego is further impoverished and the individual trapped in a vicious circle.

There are many ways in which expectation and experience may not adequately match up. Take an example that we have used before: rage associated with simple frustration. If this is noxious to the child's carers then the child may be deprived of opportunities to explore the emotion of aggression and its consequent effect on external reality. If this persists, the child will find it hard to distinguish between the fantasies they have regarding the consequences of their destructive urges (and remember here that destructiveness is an essential part of creativity) and the real consequences. If such a child's mother becomes ill, or the child's parents split up, then the child itself is apt to feel responsible. He or she will grow up terrified of aggression, have a difficulty with real creativity and, ironically, feel a sense of omnipotence that, by its effect on others, will deprive them of corrective emotional experiences.

In adult life such an individual may well end up blending an idealized form of creativity (one lacking in destructiveness) with a sense of omnipotence, and spend their time interfering in the lives of others. Many such people are attracted to becoming doctors, nurses, social workers and psychotherapists. Such people interpret any hostility shown by others in the face of their interference as evidence that these others need their help. In reality, it is their own repressed destructiveness that they are trying to push back over the edge of the cliff, not that of their patient.

Facing equal problems are those individuals driven to take the opposite path to resolve their misery. Instead of trying to adapt themselves to their distorted view of the environment, they turn inwards. Such people avoid the confusion their developing ego faces in trying to make internal expectation and external experience match up by taking their internal world as the only real thing there is. This way madness lies.

The aim of therapy is to free the patient from fixed overreliance on either the archetypal processes or the expectations of the external world. Activities essential in this development are:

Recognition – of ego-depriving patterns of behaviour along with the fantasies that have no base in reality that go along with them.

Acceptance – of the environmental failures which produced the disturbance in the archetype/ego/environment relationship.

Recovery – of the lost fragments of archetypal demands and potential, along with the related longings of the ego.

Reintegration – of the repudiated aspects of the self to form a more whole self. The external world of others can then be related to along with the internal world of the individual, in a way that builds the strength of the ego rather than forcing compromise and diminishment.

Jungian therapy has evolved somewhat during its history which means that whilst there would be broad acceptance of the above activities amongst practitioners, therapeutic technique varies widely.

Jung was himself wary of dependency and preferred to avoid reference to himself as central to the process. So, instead of concentrating on the 'here and now' aspects of the patient's interactions with him in order to understand the confusions of their inner world, he encouraged them to bring along homework in the shape of recorded dreams and thoughts, and to note down his guiding comments. He also preferred the apparent equality of patient and therapist sitting facing each other.

Many modern Jungians now tend to:

Use the couch (which was initially a Freudian device for encouraging the mind to wander).

Create a cosy, safe, predictable environment for therapy.

Accept that, within the session, the patient's interactive dependency and regression to early life is an inevitable and useful tool in the recognition and understanding of psychological disruption.

See patients up to five times a week.

Accept dreams as useful, but not demand them.

Encourage the patient's own reflections and try to understand what the patient does to disrupt this process.

'Hold' the patient emotionally to maximize their courage to be curious and explore within the safe environment of the therapy.

Avoid directly teaching the patient.

The hope is that patients will learn to reflect upon themselves in a way that is in line not only with the reality of their internal worlds, but also with the demands and opportunities of the external world. This promotes choice for an otherwise rigidly compulsive and trapped ego.

CRITICAL SUMMARY

Setting – Usually in a room set aside specifically for therapy, such as the therapist's consulting rooms or in a clinic.

Aim – Therapy aims to free the patient from overreliance on either the external world of expectation and gratification, or the internal world of rigidly held archetypes.

Technique – Using the relationship of mutuality and exploration that is fostered between the therapist and the patient, the archetypal world and expectations are explored using, as much as possible, the patient's own insights and abilities.

Good points – Analytical Psychology is painstaking and sensitive, it has the capacity, with great expense of time and effort, to dig down to the depths of the personality and re-evaluate the very earliest disruptions of the developing psyche.

Often effective for – The unbearable feeling of being stuck, hauntings from the past, non-clinical depression, and an interest in emotional growth. Problems of middle life and adjustment to old age were particular interests of Jung and are still reflected in the relevance of his therapy to these age groups.

Bad points – Can be a little narrow in its theoretical outlook – depending upon the attitude and experience of the therapist. Very time and money consuming and occasionally too intellectual for the temperament of some patients. A successful analysis may result in the patient having to come to terms with uncomfortable personal limitations. Someone considering Jungian analysis has to be prepared to exchange the air cushion of self-importance for the hard ground of ordinariness.

Seldom effective for – As might be expected, Analytical Psychology is not appropriate for crisis intervention and is less useful than some other therapies for group awareness and social skills.

40

Cost – Inevitably quite high. The reason for this is the high cost of training and overheads for the therapist and the sheer number of sessions that have to be attended and paid for.

Availability – Widely available but thin on the ground. Patients may have to be prepared to travel.

Commitment – It is possible to get short term therapy in this discipline but this is unusual. Commitment is, therefore, great. Sessions are usually three or more times a week and arranged around the holidays of patient and therapist.

Training – Takes a long time and is intensive. As with all the best psychotherapies, a fundamental part of the training is the trainee therapist's own analysis.

Further information – The Society and Association represent the spread of Jungian thinking and therapy in Britain today. *(See Resource Guide).* Anyone thinking of therapy would do well to approach both when enquiring after therapists in their area.

EXISTENTIAL THERAPY

BACKGROUND

The existential approach to personal growth is the most philosophical of those that can still be termed as psychotherapy. The background of Existential Therapy is the whole of the philosophical tradition of man, but, for those in western Europe, the emphasis is upon the writings of such as Kierkegaard (1831–55), Nietzsche (1844–1900) and Heidegger (1889–1976). The most well-known and probably most important person to develop philosophy into therapy this century is Rollo May, in the USA.

Existential Psychotherapy turns itself to the fundamental questions of what it means to be alive and where people fit into

PRINCIPLES OF PSYCHOTHERAPY

the question, and then addresses these issues with openness and receptivity. Prejudice and assumptions are risen above so that those things that have been taken for granted can be looked at afresh. Instead of an interpretation designed to fit a patient's experiences into a particular framework (as in some other therapies) Existential Therapy seeks to understand how something is experienced by the person him or herself.

THE EXISTENTIAL VIEW OF THE PERSON

Existential theory views a person not as a discrete object with a clearly defined self, but rather as a sort of transient 'thickening' in time and space. In this situation the conscious being feels troubled over the meaning of its existence: part of existence is a deep sense of anxiety or 'angst'. Dimensions of existence and experience thus become of paramount importance to the Existential Therapist. Whereas categories, labels and systems of psychological cause and effect are important to other kinds of therapy, this is not the case for Existential Psychotherapy. Here, the four important dimensions of human existence are:

Physical – The relationship we have and try to have with the substance of the world around us such as food, shelter, health and our physical ability to control ourselves and the impact of natural forces upon us. In a technological age, the equipment for this struggle is very sophisticated but the central concerns are unaltered from primitive times.

Social – The relationship we have and try to have with the people around us. Where prejudices, and the realities of economics, ethnicity and culture are key features. We have experiences on the continuums love/hate, cooperation/competition and 'part of'/'not part of', depending upon our acceptance or rejection of the influences and pressures that we encounter.

Psychological – The relationship we have and try to have with ourselves. In this dimension the personal world is created and our identity looked for. This leads to much confusion because disintegration is as common as the consolidating effect of self-affirmation. Always in the back of a person's mind is the final disintegration of death – but if we are afraid to die, we are afraid to live.

Spiritual – The relationship we have and try to have with the unknown. Faith in something beyond ourselves is the usual way in which this dimension is expressed and understood. Ultimately, if something matters to us then we matter.

THE EXISTENTIAL VIEW
OF PSYCHOLOGICAL PROBLEMS

In existential terms, contentment is found in not resisting what is truly occurring, be it pleasurable or troubling. Central to this theme is the idea of creativity, in the sense that being alive is a kind of constant metabolism in all of the above dimensions – spiritual, psychological, social and physical. The best kind of creativity is that demonstrated by small children when they unselfconsciously play with their bricks in an autonomous way, undirected by adults. For a child in this situation an essential part of the creative experience is destroying what they have built and then starting again: there is contentment and necessity in both aspects. Many adults find this free metabolic process objectionable because they have spent part or all of their life attempting to repudiate either the positive or negative aspects of the four dimensions of experience. Such individuals (and it is all of us to some extent) become stuck and unable to take in, metabolize and grow from what life, in these four dimensions, presents to us.

Comfort and contentment come not from rejecting that which is upsetting (but inevitable), but from living 'authentically' and 'truthfully'. In this way people gain experience of being able to metabolize the positive and negative parts of life and the creative and destructive parts of themselves. Discontentment and psychological ill health result from an unwillingness or inability to feed off the downs of life as well as the ups, or vice versa. When this is the case, a process of progressive isolation from key aspects of each of the various dimensions occurs: physically, we neglect ourselves; socially, we withdraw from others; psychologically, we disown parts of ourselves and spiritually we decide we know what is going on and negate the need for faith.

HOW EXISTENTIAL PSYCHOTHERAPY HELPS

The goal of this therapy is towards *personal authenticity*. This is harder than it might at first seem because the 'self' that has to become authentic is not an entity within the person – as in many other therapies – but rather a 'process'. The 'self process' requires, as we have seen, that we break our automatic habits of shutting out things in the four dimensions that we do not want, and think we do not need.

Another aspect of Existential Therapy is its dislike of rigid technique. Here we see, perhaps most clearly, that existentialism is the most philosophical of the therapies. Nevertheless there are attitudes and approaches which the therapist will quite probably adopt. Here are a few:

The naive attitude – The therapist retains an open mind.

Assumptions – The client's assumptions about themselves and the world, many of which they are not aware of, are pointed out and used to take a fresh look at apparently insoluble problems.

Vicious circles – Are revealed in order that the self-defeating and self-fulfilling expectations of low achievement can be undermined.

Facing limitations – One of the hardest things to face about oneself and about life. Nevertheless, this process is central to the sense of extreme personal honesty inherent in the existential approach.

Consequences – This involves doggedly facing the implications of personal choice and taking responsibility for the results.

Exploring personal world view – All the patient's attitudes, feelings, prejudices are explored by the therapeutic couple.

Dreams – Like fantasies and expectations of the future, dreams are explored for the information they yield about the experience of existence for the patient.

Emotions – The whole emotional spectrum is encouraged and valued as important in the process of working out what kind of person the patient is.

The aim of Existential Therapy is not to change people but to help them come to terms with themselves and life with all its paradoxes and complications. At first sight this seems to set Existential Therapy apart from other therapies, but in reality all therapies are a mixture of acceptance and personal change; indeed, neither can occur without the other. 'Cure' is not a concept that is recognized by Existential Therapy so the formal process with the therapist stops when the patient feels ready.

Setting – Usually in the therapist's consulting rooms.

Aim – To help the patient discover their own response to life and to be able to accept life's limitations and possibilities.

Technique – Exploration, through honest reflection, of the attitudes, feelings and world view of the person.

Good points – Very intellectually satisfying, flexible and widely applicable to a host of other academic disciplines such as anthropology or theology.

Often effective for – Dissatisfaction with life, interest in growing as a person, and realizing personal potential.

Bad points – Limited in its scope to deal with anxieties and neuroses based upon repressed early hurts or abuse.

Seldom effective for – Crisis, addiction, depression or group problems.

Cost – Moderately high because of the expense of sessions and the length of therapy required.

Availability – Available in most areas but thin on the ground.

Commitment – High.

Training – Available, but long and intensive.

BEHAVIOURAL THERAPY

BACKGROUND

Behavioural Therapy mushroomed in the nineteen fifties although it came into being somewhat earlier. At the beginning of this century it was found that children's phobias and unwanted behaviour could be modified using some of the techniques

described below. However it wasn't until the last forty years that a thorough scientific approach was adopted, and this, together with a greater openness in the medical profession, has helped Behavioural Therapy assume its rightful place as an effective therapy for certain problems.

HOW BEHAVIOURAL THERAPY VIEWS THE PERSON

The behavioural approach to the person is deceptively simple: people's behaviour is an indication of their psychological health and by changing their behaviour a person's health can also change. The second pillar of Behavioural Therapy is the theory of learning, which explains how behaviours are learned and sometimes unlearned. It is implicit in the behavioural view of a person that psychological health and ill health can both be learned and unlearned.

'Learning Theory' holds two models by which we acquire behaviour: *classical* and *operant conditioning*. *Classical conditioning* is that developed by Pavlov in the early part of this century. Noticing that dogs salivated at the sight of food and concluding that the link between the two was automatic, he called the food the *unconditioned stimulus* and the salivation the *unconditioned response*. He then rang a bell at the same time as presenting the food so that the sound of the bell became associated with the food in the mind of the dog. He called the bell the *conditioned stimulus* because he soon found that the dogs would salivate at the sound of the bell even in the absence of food. The salivation, because it was now conditional on the bell ringing, became the *conditioned response*.

Operant conditioning is slightly different and arose from work with cats in cages. The cat was locked in a cage where random activity meant that it would eventually, and by accident, pull a loop which would release the door and allow it to escape and so reduce its anxiety. As the cat was repeatedly locked in the cage it became quicker and quicker at escaping. This was because the favourable outcome of pulling the string 'reinforced' the string pulling behaviour. The point is that the cat's behaviour was determined by the consequence – in this case the reduction of anxiety.

Behaviourists are concerned with the individual's visible and observable behaviour and its environmental context much more, and often to the exclusion of, their emotional inner feelings or disturbed development.

THE BEHAVIOURAL THERAPY EXPLANATION OF PSYCHOLOGICAL PROBLEMS

Behavioural Therapy views symptoms as small parts of behaviour which have *maladaptive learning* at their centre. A faulty *stimulus-response link* leads to inappropriate behaviour towards a stimulus which would ordinarily be neutral and not provoke a strong reaction. The consequences of this inappropriate behaviour in turn reinforce the initial response.

Here is an example, taking a simple phobia, and putting together the theories of both *classical* and *operant* conditioning. A child visits its grandparents on a regular basis and there is a resident dog at their house. The child has naturally associated soft, furry things with pleasure – *unconditioned stimulus* is linked with *unconditioned response*. However if, when the dog is approached and petted, it becomes aggressive and starts barking loudly in the child's face then, with repeated exposure (and it may only need to be a few times) the dog becomes, in the child's mind, a *conditioned stimulus* of an *unconditioned response* – the fear of excessive noise. In time, the *conditioned stimulus* of dog-like animals becomes linked with the now *conditioned response* of fear. This is the *classical* part of the chain. The result is that the child avoids situations that induce fear, in this case

meeting dogs, and as a result the child's anxiety is reduced. This in turn reinforces the 'reward' of the child's avoidance. The whole cycle demonstrates the *operant* aspects of the *maladaptive* learnt behaviour; in this case dog-phobia.

Individuals who avoid what they experience as anxiety-ridden situations, such as exams, social activities or sexual intercourse, will be perpetuating their difficulties by depriving themselves of the opportunity to have corrective experiences. To put it in Learning Theory terms, they reinforce their own maladaptive behaviour. A 'healthier' individual will have had more positive experiences of trying to manipulate their environment and so their faith in the behavioural process of trying again and again will be reinforced.

Three other aspects of the behavioural approach are an understanding of the place of anxiety, an understanding of gratification as a way of reinforcing the undesirable behaviour, and loss of social skills:

Anxiety – is central to phobias (such as dogs, spiders, school), panic attacks, rituals (such as checking or hand washing), and sexual difficulties (such as erectile impotence or painful intercourse).

Gratification – of an appetite actually reinforces the appetite itself. If the appetite is not easily satiated then it can run away with itself. In most people hunger is easily satisfied and the pleasure of eating diminishes accordingly. For an unlucky few this is not the case and obesity results. In some others the rewards of intoxication are greater than the pleasures of clear-headedness and addiction results. This kind of appetite-based *maladaption* is also an important part of sexually deviant behaviour.

Loss of social skills – usually comes about as a consequence of repeatedly avoiding the same situations, and thus the opportunities to learn social skills. Individuals with a deficit of social skills reinforce their own maladaption and require training in social skills to link the inevitable anxiety they will face in new situations with the practical reward of a greater sense of interaction with and control over their environment.

HOW BEHAVIOURAL THERAPY HELPS

Many disorders have been found to respond to behavioural intervention. These include phobias, obsessions, tics, habits, bed-wetting, school phobia, alcoholism, antisocial behaviour, lack of assertiveness and hypochondria.

Assessment for therapy requires a behavioural analysis to be performed by the therapist and patient so that the exact difficulties can be understood and the therapy can be tailored accordingly. Behavioural analysis has three phases:

The nature of the problem. The trigger of the behaviour, the behaviour itself and the consequences are all assessed in detail so that learning theory can be applied to understanding what perpetuates the difficulty despite the fact that the patient is distressed by it.

The predictability of the various components of the difficulty is noted so that interventions can be targeted at key points in the maladaptive cycle and so that progress can be carefully monitored.

The impact of the behaviour on lifestyle, relationships and happiness is important because the therapy can be focused upon areas of greatest distress. In this way, confidence in the ability to manipulate the environment will be enhanced as much as possible and the patient will be able to take responsibility for themselves.

EXAMPLES OF BEHAVIOURAL INTERVENTION

In the case of behaviour linked with anxiety, therapy aims to break the vicious circle that avoidance of the stimulus – for example, spiders – creates, or avoidance of the environment associated with the stimulus – which in the case of spiders is any dark space. This is achieved by exposing the patient to spiders in a form that can be tolerated, even though it is mildly anxiety-provoking. The intensity of the exposure is increased progressively in steps until the anxiety diminishes to such an extent that the improvement in *environmental competence* (the ability to think about and then enter dark, and potentially spider-ridden spaces) begins to reinforce the *adaptive* behaviour, leading to a loss of fear of spiders. Relaxation techniques are sometimes used with the above 'de-sensitization' technique to make exposure to pictures, thoughts and real phobic objects more tolerable.

Obsessional behaviour, such as persistent cleaning or extreme hypochondria, requires reinforcement by the environment in order to persist. People looking for dirt will always find it so the gratification has to be interrupted: therapy blocks the cleansing act. Hypochondriacs seek constant reassurance from other people to reinforce their disease-seeking behaviour: relatives and friends are often enlisted to withhold reassurance in order to help break the reinforcement of the behaviour.

Behavioural therapy when it is applied to an appetite problem, such as obesity, involves a variety of techniques. One is *self-monitoring* – keeping a diary of eating so that improvement can be monitored (this reinforces changes in behaviour). Another is *practising normal behaviour*, such as imposing normal eating patterns. There is also *planned behaviour* – where activities such as shopping and menus are planned.

Social skills training uses training programmes broken down into progressive steps to help patients make good their personal development. Key aspects of this are starting simply and setting achievable goals (which maximizes positive reinforcement of the new behaviour early in sessions and thereby increases attendance). Training is usually in closed groups with others who all start with equal levels of functioning.

There is also a concentration on observable behaviour, for example posture, use of eyes, tone of voice, conversation techniques and use of touch, because of the non-verbal cues these give.

Behavioural techniques like those described above have been found to be helpful for a wide range of other difficulties such as panic attacks, phobias, obsessional tidying or hand washing, school phobia and delinquent behaviour.

CRITICAL SUMMARY

Setting – Most Behavioural Therapy takes place in NHS clinics with exercises being set for the patient to perform at home. Like everything else it is also available privately.

Aim – To abolish an undesirable response to a normal life stimulus and replace it with desirable behaviour.

Technique – Careful individual assessment followed by a behavioural programme modified and adapted to the specific needs of the patient.

Good points – Time-efficient: does not need a highly trained therapist. Highly adaptable and results can be easily measured.

Often effective for – Psychological difficulties where the overt behaviour is the main problem.

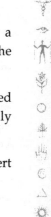

Bad points – Relatively superficial. Does not address the deeper or unseen hurts and neuroses that can be the cause of unwanted behaviour. This may result in a new unwanted behaviour surfacing or a return to the original problem.

Seldom effective for – Those emotional difficulties that clearly have their roots in past psychological disturbances, abuse or in a recent crisis.

Cost – Often free.

Availability – Widely available.

Commitment – Not high, but best results are obtained if both therapist and patient persist with the therapy, particularly in the early stages when the benefits will not outweigh the gratification of, or difficulty in, stopping the unwanted behaviour.

Training – Variable. Most NHS clinics are very good.

COGNITIVE PSYCHOTHERAPY

BACKGROUND

Cognitive Psychotherapy is an elaboration and extension of Behavioural Therapy (*see previous section*). Cognitive Therapy grew mainly from a systematic investigation of the thoughts and beliefs (known as *cognitions*) of anxious and depressed patients. Prime movers in this process were Beck, Kelly (*see Personal Construct Therapy*, page 108) and Ellis, but it was from Beck's investigations that Cognitive Therapy and its important central principle – *cognitive restructuring* – grew. His studies showed that anxious and depressed patients are preoccupied with thoughts that make their low mood worse. This led naturally to the development of a therapy that involved changing the destructive thought processes so as to raise the patient's mood. The cognitive model was developed specifically for anxiety and depression, and was not intended to serve as a full explanation of the human psyche or a multipurpose tool for behavioural change. For this reason it is unlike most of the other therapies considered in this book and although such a limitation might seem like a shortcoming, it has allowed Cognitive Therapy to remain a very easily targeted form of therapy.

HOW COGNITIVE THERAPY VIEWS THE PERSON

A person's actions are seen as being the product of the cognitive processes which affect the interpretation that an individual puts on an event or feeling, and the decisions they subsequently make. Cognitive Therapy is based upon a model of the mind and so distinguishes itself from Behavioural Therapy which does not attempt to explain the processes which control learning.

The cognitive approach can be distinguished from psychoanalytic ideas because it does not give credence to *unconscious* functioning – cognitions are *known* thoughts. In cognitive theory:

> Individuals are seen as self determining and active agents who are capable of interacting with the environment of people and things both logically and emotionally.

> Interaction is based on the decisions and judgements that a person comes to about what their senses tell them about their environment.

> The results of the cognitive processes are available to the consciousness as thoughts and images which, under certain conditions, can be changed.

Beck reasoned that a behavioural response to a situation would be determined by the interpretation of the situation made by the individual. For instance, if something is perceived as personally diminishing then they might become angry; if threatening then they try to escape, and if arousing then they become sexually active.

THE COGNITIVE THERAPY EXPLANATION OF PSYCHOLOGICAL PROBLEMS

Cognitive Therapy sees the basis of psychological ill health as a negative distortion of the available information from the environment. For instance, falling short of a personal goal – be it not getting a job, losing a mate, or failing an exam – would result in the kind of black and white thinking that children commonly adopt: 'I'm useless, there's no point in thinking about it'. An *adaptive* response is to work out what went wrong and decide whether or not to have another go, or instead to recast the original goal in a more realistic light. This requires the individual to have a good grasp of reality and to have had some experience in feeling that there is a point in taking responsibility for what happens to them.

When 'primitive' thinking – that is, 'black and white', infantile thinking – is in the ascendant, errors of logic occur in the person's information processing. Beck outlined six ways in which this happens:

Arbitrary inference – A conclusion is automatically drawn regardless of reality: 'I don't need to look at the weather, I know it's raining because I want to go for a walk.'

Selective abstraction – Focusing on a single component of the prevailing environment and ignoring other aspects. A whole personal universe is thus derived from a single star. For example, 'It's raining so everything will go wrong today.'

Overgeneralization – Taking one or two isolated but possibly traumatic instances and, from them, drawing a general rule which is applied to all situations regardless of a fit with reality: 'The people I like always turn out to be two-faced.'

Magnification and minimization – Persistent error in evaluating the real significance of events and actions: mountains are made out of molehills and molehills out of mountains.

Personalization – Events unconnected to the person are interpreted in a self-referent manner: 'There's a fire engine, I know my house is on fire'.

Absolutist, dichotomous thinking – All events or perceptions are interpreted as black or white, good or bad, perfect or useless. A depressed person would ascribe negative interpretations to themselves.

Depressed individuals show many of the attributes listed above. The situation is made worse and turned into a vicious circle because, as we have seen, these cognitive distortions of reality exclude anything that undermines the underlying assumptions of negativity towards the self. Once this sort of activity is under way the depressed person begins to fulfil their own doom-laden prophecy. They give up prematurely, teach others to think ill of them and become unappetizing companions.

THE LINK BETWEEN PAST AND PRESENT

Unlike behavioural theory, cognitive theory takes the individual's early experiences as the starting point of many adult distortions of reality, especially in cases of depression. Negative experiences, upsets, and the prevailing emotional attitudes of the carers all predispose the child to certain problems. For instance, someone with a parent or parents that are hard to

please may grow up believing that they must always do well if they are to win approval. Such a person will tend to avoid situations in which they fear failure. In this way they limit their own options. The difficulty may lie dormant until life, refusing to play by the distorted rules of the individual, presents realities that cannot be accommodated either by avoidance or perfection. Examples would be making a marriage work, rearing children, progressing in a company, fulfilling ambitions and learning new skills.

HOW COGNITIVE THERAPY HELPS

According to Cognitive theory, psychological disturbance, particularly depression, begins, as we have seen, with the faulty processing of information. This leads to false assumptions which lead to irreconcilable and debilitating frustrations. Therapy seeks to correct the original faulty interpretations and modify the assumptions, to free the patient to live more fully in the world of reality.

Modern Cognitive Therapy involves a deliberate problem-solving sequence which is not unlike that of Behavioural Therapy:

To understand fully the patient's problems.

To tailor a therapeutic strategy to the individual's needs.

To use behavioural techniques to augment and complement the individual packages of Cognitive Therapy known as *cognitive interventions*.

To assess regularly the efficacy of the treatment.

There are many therapeutic strategies. Here is a selection of some of the most often used:

Challenging underlying assumptions – The validity of the *maladaptive cognitions* are sensitively but firmly questioned. Evidence both for and against the assumptions is explored in order that the cognitions can be matched with reality.

Socratic questioning – The therapist encourages the patient to reason with them in order that the client can experience for themselves the effect of logic upon their arbitrary inferences and distorted cognitions.

Identifying automatic thoughts – The therapist helps the patient to learn to intercept the negative and automatic thoughts that initially seem to be inseparable from the triggering event. This may be an actual occurrence such as seeing a happy couple, or a triggering thought like, 'I've not got a special friend', which leads to 'I'm ugly so what's the point of trying…'

Reality testing – Once again, evidence for *maladaptive cognitions* based on automatic thoughts is subjected to cross-examination to see if it stands up to logical questioning. For instance, the logic of automatically thinking: 'So-and-so didn't phone back when I left a message so they obviously don't like me,' followed by depressive feelings, is challenged. What are the facts backing up these assumptions? Possibly none.

'De-catastrophizing' – 'Worst case' scenarios are looked at by the therapist and patient and found to be quite manageable when faced head-on. An example would be the person who ruins social occasions for themselves and others by trying to make everything perfect. Fear that they will forget something debilitates them. Therapy helps patients to come to terms with the manageability of the 'worst case' and the realistic expectation that it is unlikely to happen anyway.

Advantages and disadvantages – This involves simply making a list of the objective advantages and disadvantages concerning a difficult decision or course of action.

Cognitive Therapy aims to help the patient become aware of the *maladaptive* or disordered thought processes that are leading to their self-destructive behaviour and depression. Together, the patient and therapist examine the cognitions to see if they stand up to logical scrutiny. If they do not, it becomes increasingly difficult for the patient to adhere to them, and choice begins to be built into a person's life where previously it never existed.

CRITICAL SUMMARY

Setting – Like Behavioural Therapy, cognitive work is usually available as part of the local NHS Psychological Medicine provision. It is also widely available privately.

Aim – The aim is to improve the patient's depressive feelings and cognitions, and alter their negative self-concepts and world views.

Technique – By reasoning through the thought processes their illogicality is revealed and they are rendered less harmful and all-consuming.

Good points – Relatively easy to comprehend and make use of. Well focused for depression that does not have a large biochemical basis (*see Chapter One: Putting Words to Feelings*).

Often effective for – Only effective for depression.

Bad points – Not always long lasting in its benefits, which may imply that it is the contact with the therapist that produces a reduction in symptoms, rather than the therapy itself.

Seldom effective for – Anything other than depression.

Cost – Free from the NHS. A private session might be expected
to cost about the same as a parking ticket.

Availability – Available in most urban centres.

Commitment – A normal course would be about eight sessions
with a review and follow-up later. Clearly, anyone who is
serious about improving will attend all their sessions.

Training – Almost always of a high standard. There are good
training courses and Cognitive Psychotherapists are often
encouraging to be with.

PERSON CENTRED THERAPY

BACKGROUND

Carl Rogers (1902–1987) was responsible for the creation of **Person Centred Therapy**. He believed that his most revolutionary
discovery was the existence of a kind of wholeness at the heart
of the personality, and that man's deepest nature is positive and
constructive both in terms of itself and in relation to others.

Interestingly, as a young man Rogers began by training for
the Christian ministry. However, he moved away from it, and
created a therapy that has at its centre a belief that many think is
opposite to the Christian doctrine, which holds that man is sinful and corrupt until saved and redeemed. Rogers' belief was
in the innate wholeness and goodness of human nature.
Because of this stance, Person Centred Therapy stands on a
very different part of the historical development chart from
those therapies that have grown up directly from the Freudian
tradition. Rogers believed that inside every individual who
came for help there lay a 'real person' who was, to a greater
or lesser extent, dormant and undisfigured beneath the
fears, worries and blind alleys that bogged him or her down in

everyday life. Person Centred Therapy (PCT) is what is usually meant by *counselling* and in many situations the two terms can safely be used interchangeably. However there is a tendency for many other kinds of therapy to be referred to as *counselling*, so it is always advisable to check exactly what someone means when they use the word.

HOW PERSON CENTRED THERAPY VIEWS THE PERSON

Person Centred Therapy has, as a central assumption, the idea that the real self can be reached out for, awakened and encouraged to stumble into the light. Persons are viewed as having at their core a capacity for *actualizing* which is both powerful and directional. Like a lode-stone that always points to magnetic north, people are seen as always trying to move towards becoming who they really are. Even if the emotional environment they experience inside or outside themselves makes it hard to move forward, this part of our humanness is thought to be as strong as a seed trapped under an asphalt path. It will grow and it will break through.

THE PERSON CENTRED THERAPY EXPLANATION OF PSYCHOLOGICAL PROBLEMS

PCT views everyone as having a *self-concept* which is developed during life and which may or may not closely match the *self*, which is the actualizing part of the personality. Where a person's self-concept corresponds closely to their self there will be a good link between who they actually are and who they try to be.

Such individuals as these seldom experience much of an 'asphalt path' to break through and are moving towards being what Rogers called *fully functioning persons*. The fully functioning person exhibits five key traits:

They are comfortable with new ideas, and experiences.

They have the ability to take responsibility for their own actions.

They are free to make choices in life that feel right for them.

They are capable of lateral thinking and of flexible, creative responses to problems.

They are focused on what is happening in the present.

Such a person is confident that they are 'okay' in their *self*. They are genuinely self-confident. Such a person will be well integrated into the society around them but will not necessarily need to be conformist in their approach or their behaviour.

In Rogerian terms the problems start when the *self-concept* is at odds with the *self*. The individual becomes preoccupied with the struggle to maintain the shaky edifice of the false self-concept which is constantly under threat from the natural inclinations and desires of their self, which lies buried in the foundations of their erroneous self-concept. Thus the five features that characterize the poorly functioning person are:

They are threatened by new ideas, people and experiences.

They look to others to take responsibility for them.

They make decisions based upon what others will think.

They hold inflexible, dogmatic opinions which appear to them to be justified.

They are haunted by the past and fearful of the future.

Most people lie somewhere between the two extremes of fully and poorly functioning person.

THE LINK BETWEEN PAST AND PRESENT

Rogers and his followers believe that positive regard and approval from others is the principal need of the developing infant. Early in life the *self* is inevitably in the ascendant because the *self-image* has only just begun to form. This is why babies are unselfconscious creatures living in the present moment and driven by their immediate appetites and desires.

For every child, the main emotional activity will take place between the self and the part of the world around them that is discovered to be the best source of positive regard and approval. In most cases this is the parents or parent. If approval is only given when the child behaves in ways that conform to the expectations of the carer, then conflicts will arise in the child between its need for approval and the desires of the self to fulfil itself. It is in this setting that, in order to try and ease the tension, inaccurate self-concepts develop. For instance, it is quite natural, from time to time, for children to become enraged with their carers. If this rage is unacceptable to the carer then they will tend – unconsciously or deliberately – to withdraw their positive regard. The child will eventually learn that it can not afford to show rage and must respond by developing an 'I don't get angry' *self-concept*. The *self* is thus buried a little more.

To a certain extent these sort of conflicts can be tolerated and resolved. However, if the anti-self injunctions imposed by carers or significant others are too numerous and profound, then the individual will feel despair and helplessness in the face of continued prompting by the self. When this level of disturbance occurs the self becomes mistaken for the actual cause of the despair and is then attacked and discarded as an unwanted or bad part of the person.

Individuals in this position find it hard to make anything of themselves – to *actualize* – because they can never get enough approval or acceptance from others to make them feel good enough about themselves. Nothing from outside can ever replace the void once occupied by the banished self, and yet the only option they have left is to try to get what they need from others over and over again.

HOW PERSON CENTRED THERAPY HELPS

The relationship that the client is encouraged to have with the therapist is one that challenges false self-concepts. It does this in two main ways. Firstly, by valuing experiences that do not fit the false aspects of the self-concept and secondly, by attempting to have a relationship with the buried self. The personal approach of the therapist forms the backbone of the process. This has three aspects:

Unconditional positive regard.

Not being judgmental.

Empathy – as distinct from sympathy, meaning climbing into someone else's shoes and feeling what it is like to be them.

The therapeutic relationship moves through three phases:

Trust – where the client discovers that their false self-concepts are not necessary to receive approval and positive regard from the therapist.

Intimacy – where the self is revealed as the client regains awareness of their deeper and more genuine experiences.

Mutuality – the maturing phase in which self-disclosure by the therapist increases.

It is important to remember that underlying Person Centred Therapy is Rogers' belief in the innate capacity and desire of the self to *actualize*. Thus therapists need only provide the right environment of genuineness, acceptance and empathy for growth to occur. In essence, PCT is simply a way of 'being' with another person that allows them to become who they really are. Although there are, as we have seen above, theoretical assumptions and therapeutic strategies used in PCT, it is the attitude and personality of the therapist that is crucial to the process.

CRITICAL SUMMARY

Setting – Because of its ubiquitous nature, PCT can be found in many settings: counselling centres, voluntary agencies, churches, community self-help groups and even on the telephone.

Aim – To release the client from the burden of trying to be who they are not, and to help them find choices for living with a greater sense of reality, in themselves and in their relationships.

Technique – By adopting an open and mutual stance in relation to the client, the therapist helps make it possible for difficult truths about the client to be recognized and explored. PCT therapists do not give advice, but rather make it plain that they believe in the client's capacity for helping themselves, given the right encouragement.

Good points – PCT is a gentle and thought provoking therapy that encourages a sense of appropriate self-worth, as well as being flexible enough to support people as they consider who they are and what they want to do with their lives.

Often effective for – General dissatisfaction with life, difficulties in coming to terms with painful past events, understanding of difficulties in relationships, bereavement, and adjustment to illness or change in life circumstances.

Bad points – Does not usually address deeply repressed unconscious memories or conflicts and so tends to re-enforce coping defences rather than getting to the causes. Nevertheless, the relief of symptoms can often be pronounced and long lasting.

Seldom effective for – Depression, phobias, alcoholism or eating disorders.

Cost – Varies from free of charge through donations to moderate fees.

Availability – Widespread.

Commitment – Varies according to the contract made with the therapist at the beginning of therapy.

Training – Training of various levels and quality is available. The best therapists are those who are affiliated to a reliable organization.

TRANSACTIONAL ANALYSIS

BACKGROUND

Transactional Analysis is associated with the name of Eric Berne. With his theoretical roots in Psychoanalysis, Berne developed the interactive elements of the inner emotional world of the individual into a user-friendly and widely accessible language. The language of Transactional Analysis – *parent*, *adult*, *child*, *script*, and so on – uses familiar words, but defines their meaning for its own use. The effect of this is that the novice can very quickly pick up some of the vocabulary and start stringing meaningful sentences together. Partly because of this and partly because Transactional Analysis takes patterns of inner-world functioning and extends them into the way we try to relate to one another, Transactional Analysis is a powerfully educative psychotherapy. The therapy nearly always takes place in groups which meet regularly.

Like Rogers, Berne believed that we are inherently oriented towards making the best of ourselves. However, he recognized one of the fundamental tragedies of individual lives and perhaps of mankind in general – that our destructive potential overwhelms us and therefore we cannot fulfil ourselves without help.

HOW TRANSACTIONAL ANALYSIS VIEWS THE PERSON

At the heart of Transactional Analysis is the notion that our personality is made up of three elements or *ego states*:

Parent – the feelings, attitudes and behaviour patterns that resemble those of a parental figure.

Adult – the feelings, attitudes and behaviour patterns that are genuinely one's own and are in step with the reality of our environment and our relationships in the present.

Child – the feelings, attitudes and behaviour patterns that are 'action replays' of one's early life.

Generally, the *parental* and *child* behaviour patterns are automatic and feel, to the person performing them, appropriate to the present. In other words the knowledge that a present relationship with, for example, a boyfriend, is being led at least in part as if it were the original (and perhaps traumatically disappointing) relationship with the father, is not known. It is unconscious. One of the most powerful aspects of Transactional Analysis is that it provides us with a way of understanding why we do, feel and believe things that are false about ourselves and others, while holding these convictions with a certainty that our perceptions of ourselves and others are correct.

THE TRANSACTIONAL ANALYSIS EXPLANATION OF PSYCHOLOGICAL PROBLEMS

At the centre of Berne's explanation for human troubles is the notion of *scripting*. Scripting occurs when the child, usually in response to a parental shortcoming, represses his or her own capacity for spontaneity, awareness and intimacy in the developmental phase. In this way decisions that have been made as a child in the interest of psychological comfort or survival, affect the grown-up person in everyday life. These decisions, such as avoiding expressing true feelings or not objecting when hurt, have been made with the inadequate information and experience of the child. More recently this whole cycle of disadvantage has been formed by TA therapists into the *Racket System*, which aims to help us understand the link between our inner psychological functioning and our relations with others. The Racket System has a set of linked elements:

Script beliefs – These are self-limiting beliefs about oneself, important others, and life in general which have been shaped by early decisions such as those described above.

Repressed feelings – The impulses, attitudes and feelings repressed as a consequence of the earlier *script* decisions.

Rackety displays – The behaviours and ways of interacting with others that demonstrate the distorted inner attitudes and emotions of the person concerned.

Reinforcing memories – The memories (accurate or distorted) which someone collects to reinforce their basic script decisions and perpetually justify their grievances against those

they feel have let them down. Further memories will be added as time goes on because of the way in which others respond in the face of, for instance, an aggressive or victim status that may be adopted.

Search for strokes – The child's self-imposed limitations are perpetuated because the adult continues to search for what Berne has called *positive strokes*. Positive strokes are affirmation and approval which the person goes on seeking. *Negative strokes*, or criticisms, are avoided in the same way.

HOW TRANSACTIONAL ANALYSIS HELPS

Language is fundamental to the exploration of ideas between two people. Berne intuitively understood that if he could create an easily grasped and memorable language of the way we feel inside and the way we try to relate to each other then people would spontaneously want to explore their inner emotional world.

The first aim of the therapy is to teach some of the language to the newcomer. This creates a means of dialogue, the tools to explore and describe feelings, attitudes and behaviour and – very importantly – a realistic sense of 'can do'. Thus Transactional Analysis has incorporated within it the devices necessary to undermine those feelings, attitudes and behaviours which make emotional reflection so difficult: despair, hopelessness, suspicion, loneliness and avoidance. These are replaced with the invitation to be hopeful, explorative, responsible and part of something good.

Taking the principle that the best way to learn a language is to use it, TA then diagnoses the ego states, using four methods. These are:

Behavioural – The words, voice, tone, gestures, expressions, posture and attitudes of the client are observed and explored for their hidden meaning.

Social – The way in which the client responds to others and is, in turn, responded to, is observed and explored for its meaning.

Historical – The client and therapist look back to identify actual experiences that did occur in every ego state – particularly those of the child.

Phenomenological (what it feels like to be you) – self-examination leads to an understanding of ego states.

Autonomy, one of the principal attributes of the adult ego state, is another central aim of TA psychotherapy, and is built up either individually with a therapist, or in a group. Autonomy shows itself in the increase of three tendencies in the client:

Awareness – Being able to experience the perceptions of the present as if for the first time, untransformed by the destructive past experiences embodied in the *scripts*.

Spontaneity – the tendency to acknowledge and respond to feelings in a way that is genuine, and not intended to produce a particular effect on oneself or others.

Intimacy – a combination of awareness and spontaneity in the social context which results in spontaneous, non game-playing relations which are not prescribed or influenced by *parent-child scripts*.

Once the therapist has come to a working diagnosis of the condition of the parent, adult and child ego states and the way in which they interact for good and ill, it becomes possible to understand the particular therapeutic needs of the client. Strategies used to get to this state are:

Motivation – Accepting the reality of the limitations in the way the existing ego state functions creates curiosity to learn about Transactional Analysis.

Awareness – Working with the therapist the client finds out what needs to be changed. This is a challenging process which involves confronting *parent* material which is demanding or undermining, and *child scripts* which are debilitating.

Treatment Contract – If this stage is reached the *adult* will have become sufficiently available to the client and therapist for a statement of therapeutic goals to be made. These will be constantly referred to.

'De-confusing' the *child* ego state – The client feels safe enough in the therapeutic environment to explore and name the unmet needs of childhood, which have been denied in the process of creating the scripts necessary for psychological or physical survival.

'Re-decision' – The point, which may last for weeks or months, in which earlier life decisions made in the child ego state and turned into *scripts* are altered. This is achieved by the adult ego state which has by now gained understanding and strength.

Relearning – 'Re-decisions' are practised in the supportive context of the therapist or therapist and group so that they become integrated into and change the feelings, attitudes and behaviour of the client in a lasting way.

Termination – An assessment of goals, celebration of success, and separation from the therapist. Finally, true autonomy.

CRITICAL SUMMARY

Setting – Community centres, adult education centres and, less commonly, specialized premises or the therapist's home.

Aim – Increased awareness and personal choice in relations with others and in attitudes to oneself.

Technique – Nearly always in groups with theory and practice: it is an educative but experiential approach.

Good points – Very accessible, with a rapid sense of real progress, often well-taught and run, and has many practical applications to everyday life.

Often effective for – The compulsion to repeat, an interest in growing, problems in groups, work relations, and problems with other family members.

Bad points – Is prone to impart a false sense of personal mastery by giving the client the illusory sense that they now have a deep understanding of others. TA can become an end in itself.

Seldom effective for – Deeper underlying hurts from the past, crisis situations, depression, or specific difficulties such as eating disorders or sexual abuse as a child.

Cost – Usually very reasonable, especially if in the context of a larger organization such as a church or education authority.

Availability – Widespread.

Commitment – Definitely required (groups should not be missed), but usually of short duration, say eight weeks at a time.

Training – Good training is available with an emphasis on professionalism and accreditation. Ideally your therapist should be accredited to the Institute of Transactional Analysis and have his or her competence endorsed by them.

GESTALT THERAPY

BACKGROUND

Gestalt ideas were formally built into a psychotherapy by Fritz Perls and his collaborators in the period following the Second World War. For Perls, Psychoanalysis failed to 'scratch him where he itched'. Perls was a very visceral 'in contact' sort of person who founded a therapy that invests both the mind and body with equal importance. We can, perhaps, imagine the young Perls thrashing about with exasperation whilst he tried to lie still and *free associate* on his psychoanalyst's couch.

Perls's viscerality, dynamism, charisma and no-nonsense confrontational approach has affected **Gestalt Therapy** for both good and ill. His permissive personality, along with his unusual intellect and perceptions, meant that besides being a compelling evangelist for his beliefs, he was elevated to guru status by others. Many would-be practitioners, lacking his intellectual grasp and integrity, imitated instead his flamboyant and confrontational style. For a time this gave Gestalt a reputation for being an indulgent and anti-intellectual therapy. Happily the equilibrium is now largely restored and there are many capable therapists around. Gestalt Therapy is nearly always done in groups.

HOW GESTALT VIEWS THE PERSON

The Gestalt view of the person has a distinctly evolutionary flavour to it. Individuals are seen as organisms interacting with their immediate environment in a way that allows them to *self-actualize*. An amoeba or sea squirt, being a simple organism, has little trouble *self-actualizing* (being who or what they truly are): as they become aware of their needs they grade these needs in terms of urgency and adjust their approach to the environment in order to get them met. The basic idea of human self-actualization is exactly the same but, of course, more complex. Gestaltists believe that, in the first instance, we sense and feel with our senses and intuitions. Next, by attending to these impressions we become *aware* and so experience a *need*. The stronger or more urgent the need, be it physical, spiritual, relational or psychological, the more it stands out from the background noise of the senses flooding in. Following this the healthy person, or organism, recognizes the choices available and creatively adjusts to meet their needs.

THE GESTALT EXPLANATION OF PSYCHOLOGICAL PROBLEMS

Gestalt sees a disruption in *awareness* and *contact* as the basis of a person's (or organism's) unhappiness. When things are going well, *awareness* – which is not the same as thinking – develops in the maturing person as an inevitable consequence of their sensing and responding to their needs. For this reason awareness can only be a 'here and now' activity. *Contact*, or being fully in touch, follows on from this and is the person's capacity to be simultaneously in contact with the reality of what is going on inside themselves (in a physical, spiritual, psychological and relational sense) and in the world around them.

When things have gone wrong, awareness and contact are disrupted so that the person lives less and less as a 'here and now' organism and has trouble at what is called the *contact boundary*. The contact boundary is the place where 'me' – the individual – ends, and everyone else begins. Gestalt psychotherapy recognizes three main ways in which this boundary is disrupted: projection, introjection, and retroflection.

Projection involves the movement of the contact boundary outward into the environment of other people and their individual 'feelings worlds'. The result is that an individual can come to believe that feelings which are actually their own but are unwelcome are not their responsibility. For example, I may believe that 'He makes me angry,' or 'He doesn't like me,' when in fact my anger is my responsibility, and I don't like him but can not admit it.

Introjection occurs when the individual moves their contact boundary inwards. In 'organismic' terms the person feels overwhelmed by the environment and just takes things in without digesting and metabolizing the bits they really need, and turning them into genuine 'bits' of themselves. For example, if someone grows up in a family where anger is not allowed by one or more parents, then the whole issue of anger and rage, and the constructive and appropriate use of this emotion, does not get digested. The result is a child who tries to behave as if he or she does not get angry. The contact boundary is thus drawn in as the parent's *projection* is *introjected*. The reader will be able to appreciate how this process compromises the 'here and now' awareness of the developing person and their capacity to get their needs met. Put simply: the spanner of anger has been removed from their tool box.

Retroflection is when someone mistakes a part of themselves for the environment, and conducts a 'dialogue' with that part in an attempt to get their needs met without relation to others. When we abuse ourselves in some way, such as starving ourselves, hitting ourselves or depriving ourselves of sleep, we are usually failing to acknowledge aggressive impulses towards our environment.

Perls and his followers believe that these destructive ripples are set up in early life. If the spontaneous development of our capacities to be aware, meet needs and regulate the contact boundary are frustrated often enough, then a child will grow up with repressed feelings, repressed physicality, disturbed relationships and unmet spiritual yearnings. They are frustrated and frustrating people. We are all at least a little like this. Cycles of disadvantage are thought to be set up early in life and are subsequently fed and encouraged during the rest of life by the energy that results from them. For example, the person who pretends that they do not get angry will occasionally build up a backlog of unacknowledged rage which suddenly explodes, apparently at something trivial, like the minor disobedience of a child. The result is, for that individual, a demonstration of the destructiveness of their anger, as the shame they subsequently feel endorses the need they feel to further rigorously repress their anger, and so on again and again. If we reflect for a moment the effect this will have upon the child at whom the explosion was aimed, we can appreciate how these cycles of disadvantage get passed down the generations.

The term used to described what happens to needs that remain unmet is *unfinished business*. Unfinished business clogs and constipates the organism. In this unfulfilled condition individuals become dissatisfied with life and lacking in drive (because the excitement and pleasure that comes from their 'here and now' awareness, and the meeting of their needs has been largely lost). They are driven to impress others or make others envious in order to replace their lost sense of purpose and potency.

HOW GESTALT THERAPY HELPS

Gestalt Psychotherapy aims to finish the *unfinished business* and through the experience of this process enable individuals to operate in the 'here and now'. People seeking help often want their therapist to be a kind of expert on whom they can be dependent. Gestaltists are suspicious of this tendency and encourage others to become experts on themselves.

Therapy sessions usually take place in groups and rely upon the innate capacity of the human organism to develop spontaneously. Therapy simply speeds this process up. In a way, Gestalt Therapy is rather like allowing a series of little life crises to happen to you so that you are forced to face up to things. The difference is that these occur in a safe and supportive, if at times uncomfortable and confrontational, environment. A competent therapist will help the client to see the ways in which they are sabotaging their own awareness, perhaps by damming up energy or depriving him or herself of an environment that will meet their needs. Once this is plain and inescapable then it becomes possible to look at the *contact boundary* disruptions that keep this process going.

This is best demonstrated with a vignette of the sort of thing that happens in a typical session:

John told the group that he wanted to work on the difficulty he was experiencing in taking criticism and took the 'hot seat' – the floor in the middle of the circle. Working on the Gestalt notion that energy is often trapped in the *resisting part* of a person rather than the part that is apparently aware of wanting help, the therapist directed the group to give John only compliments. Over and over again they praised him and told him in turn all the things they liked and admired about him. This was unexpectedly very uncomfortable for him. Soon John became tearful and shouted at the others to stop.

John came to realize that his awareness of his need for praise, admiration and encouragement from others had been blocked because he had despaired of getting any from his father, who, it emerged, had been cold and distant and whom he had always admired and looked up to. The therapist had realized that John knew where he was with criticism because it is what he expected from others – his *introjection* of 'you are not good enough' – but that in the area of encouragement he was, without knowing it, on his own. He had, from early on, resorted to affirming and praising himself – *retroflection*.

The deep-down realization of this disruption to his awareness and contact boundaries was the beginning of John's realization that others had something to offer him other than criticism and that he could not manage without their support.

This use of the 'opposite' by the therapist is one of the hallmarks of Gestalt therapy.

CRITICAL SUMMARY

Setting – Any suitable space where others are not going to be disturbed and the group can maintain its privacy. (Gestalt can get noisy!)

Aim – To free the individual from the *unfinished business* of the past and enable them to live with rich emotional diversity in the present.

Technique – In groups, with a therapist taking the lead and steering the proceedings. Each member takes it in turn to be in the 'hot seat' (the centre of the circle) to work on a particular problem with the help of the other members and the therapist.

Good points – Exciting and provoking. It is relatively easy to grasp the basic idea in a few sessions, enter the group experience and gain a new view of old problems.

Often effective for – The compulsion to repeat, dissatisfaction with life, interest in growing and problems in work and social groups.

Bad points – Gestalt therapists tend not to recognize the fact of and power of *transference*. This means that when a patient mistakes them (emotionally) for an important person in their past – mother or father – the therapist may mishandle the situation and leave the patient in a worse condition than before. Special care should be taken to avoid therapists who might have a secret desire to control and manipulate others – the 'guru' syndrome.

Seldom effective for – Deeper underlying hurts that require a therapy that understands and uses *transference*, such as Psychoanalysis. Gestalt is not practical for crisis intervention, depression or specific difficulties such as addictive behaviour or phobias.

Cost – Good Gestalt Psychotherapy is sometimes expensive but this is offset by the fact that the cost is spread throughout the group.

Availability – Genuine Gestalt Psychotherapy is not as widespread as it might on first enquiry seem. It is one of those therapies prone to incorporation in the techniques of so-called 'eclectic' (a bit of everything) therapists. Nevertheless, it is available in most large towns and cities.

Commitment – As with any group, sessions are not to be missed. They usually last about two hours and happen once or twice a week for a term.

Training – Standards of training are slowly improving, although the somewhat anti-establishment attitudes of some practitioners has undoubtedly slowed this process down. There is no formally recognized accreditation although this situation is changing all the time. When considering Gestalt Psychotherapy it is wise to go to someone with an established local reputation who is also known to the Gestalt Centre or the Gestalt Psychotherapy Training Institute.

PSYCHODRAMA

BACKGROUND

Psychodrama is a group therapy developed by J. L. Moreno (1892–1974) in which personality, interpersonal relationships, conflicts surrounding feelings, and emotional problems are explored by means of dramatic methods. Moreno was brought up in Vienna where he studied medicine, philosophy and the arts. During his twenties he led improvised play groups with children in the municipal parks, which developed into the Theatre of Spontaneity. It is fairly easy to see why there are similarities between the techniques of Psychodrama and the exercises used by theatrical companies to enrich their interpretation of an author's work. One revealing anecdote told by Moreno is of an actress in the Theatre of Spontaneity who, although she played gentle and innocent roles on stage, was a tartar in the home. When he discovered this, Moreno gave her more aggressive and insensitive characters to play, with the result that she became better behaved elsewhere.

In his early thirties Moreno emigrated to the USA where he fused together the idea of working in groups – it is widely believed that he coined the term *group therapy* – and a theatrical exploration of the emotional world of the individual, and his or her relations with others. Subsequently this became known as Psychodrama.

HOW PSYCHODRAMA VIEWS THE PERSON
AND THEIR PSYCHOLOGICAL PROBLEMS

In most of the other descriptions of psychotherapies in this book, I have made a distinction, albeit occasionally rather arbitrarily, between the view that the given theory holds of the individual, and how that person might develop emotional difficulties. With Psychodrama this distinction would be counterproductive because they are seen as one and the same thing. Here I shall assume that they are the same thing, so I have relaxed my rules and put them together. Thus the description matches the therapy.

The mainstay of the Psychodramatic view is the idea of *roles* and *role-playing*. These familiar terms that we use everyday were also invented by Moreno himself. *Roles* are predictable patterns of observable behaviour that occur in particular social situations. The complexity and variety of the roles that we play are an illustration of the complexity of the world we live in. Roles such as patient, mother, sister, uncle, lover, doctor, priest, teacher, leader, victim are all quite familiar. In real life, we play the roles for real and to the dictates of family and society, and we can not play around with them because there would be serious consequences for us and others. Two examples of this would be firstly, *within role* where, for example, a priest comes right out at a funeral service and says that in his opinion the deceased is going straight to hell without passing go: the priest has stayed a priest, but been destructive within that role. Secondly, *across role* where a priest breaks his vows of celibacy (which are partly a promise to stay *in role*) and takes on the added role of sexual lover.

In neurotic situations, where repressed or hidden wishes or memories create conflict between reality and what is allowed to be known or desired, one or more of the individual's roles will be in conflict. This is the case even when the roles are imaginary or only partially grounded in reality. An example would be the person who feels that they are the leader or victim in a social group. Another example is the son who feels unwittingly compelled to play the role of conquering hero and high achiever for his needy or unfulfilled mother, and victimized or bullied failure for his overbearing father. Psychodrama is a complex and effective system for 'conceptualizing' the individual's neuroses. It is a therapy which rapidly helps patients to gain a sense of their relations to others and their attitude to themselves.

HOW PSYCHODRAMA HELPS

By combining theatre, a controlled and safe group setting and role-playing, Psychodrama allows the patients in the group to take it in turn to re-enact and explore their neurotic conflicts and emotional disturbances. The particular group member who is being focused upon is referred to as the *protagonist* whilst the therapist is known as the *director*. The group, about eight people, will meet in closed sessions for up to two hours at a time and may well devote the whole of one session to the 'drama' of one individual. Everyone else soon becomes involved as *dramatis personae* in the action. As an illustration we can take the example of John, who we met in the section on Gestalt Therapy.

John tells the group that he has difficulty with criticism, even when it is well meant. An incident when he was a boy comes to mind in which he was given a boat kit by his parents. He had wanted the kit very much and did his best to make it as well as he could to please his father, who had resisted the purchase because he thought John was too young. With the director's help, the protagonist, John, assembled the company into the main players and re-enacted the incident. There was a father and mother, a younger sister and the so-called *auxiliary ego* – someone else playing John as well as John himself. Other group members looked on and related what was going on to their own lives. John's *auxiliary ego* became very distressed and angry when his father criticized his model for not being made well enough. John himself felt humiliated and crushed and discarded the boat. In a spontaneous gesture, the woman playing his mother rushed over to comfort him, but he shrugged her away. Mother and father then started to argue while his sister cried and John was left in confusion. By responding to what had happened, discussing it with other group members and trying alternative outcomes, John was able to explore the fact that his difficulty with criticism was based on his denial of his need for encouragement and support: he had always managed to do without it.

Psychodrama has rules and techniques which, when brought to bear on the action, bring about greater awareness of reality and choice for change.

Here are some of the rules:

Action – Conflicts are acted out and not just talked about.

Here and now – Regardless of when the incident actually happened, the action takes place in the 'here and now'.

Subjectivity – The patient must try to act out the truth as it is *felt*. Thinking about what it means comes later.

Maximum expression – All important expressions, comments and actions are given prominence and not played down.

Inward movement – The director ensures that the Psychodrama starts off with less traumatic material and moves towards deeper and more troublesome areas when the individual and the group have learnt to trust one another.

Patient choice – Although the director helps where necessary, the belief is that the protagonist knows who they want to play a particular part and what they want these people to do in the drama.

Patient 'inexpressiveness' is accepted – The patient has permission to be as unresponsive and numb as they want to be at any given time.

Interpretation – In most other therapies interpretation is verbal; in Psychodrama it is often expressed by action: the director, and possibly the protagonist or other group member, will modify the drama in some way to reveal a hidden emotion, motivation or meaning.

Three part procedure – Psychodrama sessions consist of three parts: the *warm-up*, the *action* and the *post-action* discussion by the group.

Identification with the Protagonist – Others must support the protagonist so that they are not left isolated with their conflict or insights.

Role-playing – The protagonist must be prepared to take the role of all those with whom he is meaningfully related in the drama.

Flexibility – The director must trust the Psychodramatic process as the ultimate arbiter and guide of the therapeutic process.

Here are some of the techniques used:

Soliloquy – The portrayal by 'side dialogues' and 'side actions' of hidden thoughts and feelings, which run in parallel with overt thoughts and feelings. (This technique is also used in mainstream theatre and pantomime).

Self-presentation – The protagonist presents not only himself but also all the other characters in turn, just as he perceives them. This is often a very useful way of loosening up a session so that others can join in.

Self-realization – The protagonist, with the aid of a few auxiliary egos, enacts the story of his life.

Double – The patient portrays himself but also sees himself being portrayed simultaneously by someone else. The novelty of seeing himself, and the inevitable differences in the enactments of the other group member, reveal to him hidden aspects of his own behaviour.

Mirror – Mirroring does not happen simultaneously with the re-enactment, but is watched by the protagonist. The mirror may exaggerate aspects at the instruction of the director to help make a point.

Role reversal – The protagonist switches roles with one of the other group members who is playing, for instance, his father.

Dream presentation – The patient enacts a dream instead of describing it.

As the sessions progress, different group members get the chance to enact their own dramas and take part in those of others. Problems of emotion, neurotic conflict and personality are looked at from new angles and a sense of personal mastery is achieved. The role of the director is arduous as he or she has to know the best time to interfere and when to leave well alone. Psychodrama is so intense and absorbing that everyone concerned, whether involved in the drama or not, is learning, responding and comparing for themselves.

Setting – Psychodrama needs a warm, comfortable and preferably quite large space in which to operate. It must be private and free from interruption. Occasionally the luxury of a specially built stage area is available.

Aim – By dramatizing memories and emotional conflicts insight is gained, with emotional relief as the goal.

Technique – Group members take it in turn to arrange others into reconstructions of traumatic or conflict-ridden events in their past. With help from the director, aspects of their past – and the attitudes that result from these in the present – are examined from new angles and different outcomes are rehearsed.

Good points – Psychodrama is an entertaining and provocative exercise in which to be involved because of the way the group share the experience at a moment of great vulnerability. There are many knock-on effects in terms of social skills and relationships beyond the undoubted beneficial effects of the therapy.

Often effective for – Psychodrama is especially effective for coming to terms with past difficulties and turning them from a way of life into memories. It equips people with a structure and language with which to examine why they feel stuck, dissatisfied, or on the edge of social and family groups.

Bad points – Despite the claims of its founder, J. L. Moreno, Psychodrama is not the last word in psychotherapy. Although it does have undoubted power and efficacy it is possible for someone to hide, albeit unwittingly, from much of their inner emotional world, and even to strengthen their defences against reality if they are not confronted by the process or the director.

Seldom effective for – Crisis, substance abuse, phobia and depression are not suitably treated with Psychodrama.

Cost – The cost is reasonable due to the group nature of the therapy.

Availability – High quality Psychodrama is not very common but is widely spread. It is occasionally available under the auspices of the NHS.

Commitment – This is high, as in all closed groups. Group sessions tend to be of a limited number, for instance eight consecutive weeks, or as a one-off weekend conference.

Training – This varies rather in depth. Unfortunately, Psychodrama techniques often get used by individuals with limited experience. It is best to make sure of the affiliations of your therapist and check them out; any *bona fide* therapist will expect you to do this.

GROUP PSYCHOTHERAPY

BACKGROUND

The use of groups in psychotherapy mushroomed following the First World War, but the beneficial effects of groups have been around much longer – religious communities and extended family gatherings or funeral wakes being a few examples. At the turn of the century, a doctor named Joseph Pratt brought together groups of patients with tuberculosis to instruct and encourage them. He noticed that their recovery was enhanced by their effect upon one another. Later, some innovative psychiatrists who were drafted into the British army experimented in groups with emotional aspects of shell shock, or war neurosis, to great effect. Several of these workers were also psychoanalytically trained, and were able to understand and respond to what was happening as if it were a kind of multiplied version of the one-to-one relationship of classical analysis. Thus was born **Group Analysis**. At the same time, the humanist movement in the USA experimented with the group phenomenon and gave birth to Gestalt, Transactional Analysis, Encounter, and many more (*see diagram on page 3*).

So much is now understood about the unconscious life of groups that the concept has been extended to affect management strategies in industry and inpatient care of psychotics.

Groups are rather more often the setting of a particular school, tradition or theory of Psychotherapy than the point of the whole therapy itself. For this reason I shall discuss the concept in a way that recognizes that group influences and insights run through many therapies, as well as specific group therapies themselves.

THERAPEUTIC PHENOMENA COMMON TO ALL GROUPS

There are a group of factors that have been found to be common to therapeutic groups regardless of their theoretical or technical position:

Cohesiveness – The feeling of belonging to and being accepted by the group. The security engendered by cohesiveness is essential to the process of curiosity and self-revelation.

Interaction – Sooner or later, no matter how hard they try not to, group members eventually behave in the group just as they do in the rest of life. By observing their own and each other's ways of behaving, their awareness and insight is increased.

Universality – Members discover that others are very similar to them in feelings and actions. This counters the fear of being singled out for criticism and leads to trust and sharing.

Hope – Group members encourage one another by the simple fact that when one person is feeling discouraged others will keep things going.

Altruism – People helping each other through feedback or support builds self-esteem.

Guidance – Either by example, or directly, members make suggestions to one another which can be discussed or responded to on mutual ground. This is often a new experience for those who have either been used to being told what to do, or to telling others what to do.

Vicarious learning – In a group where individuals are attending to one another, every time one person experiments with an idea or reveals a difficulty everyone else has the chance to learn from it. Each person responds to the difficulty in their own way.

Self-disclosure – It is an assumption that self-disclosure is somehow beneficial. Crying and getting angry are, for instance, quite dramatic. They show that 'something is going on'. On their own such things do not constitute psychotherapy; the response and experiences surrounding the dramatic emotional occurrences in groups can do.

Corrective experience – Groups are often like families (the first group anyone experiences) and can provide members with the opportunity to correct lifelong assumptions about being with others. Sometimes, of course, their worst fears are confirmed.

Dependency – Anxiety is at its highest when a group initially forms. People want to know what is expected of them, who the 'leader' is and what the 'rules' are. They may eventually find that they want to be free of such things, but to start with the group is very likely to be dependent upon the identified leader to provide the answers. If it is not clear who the leader is, the group will try to make one. If there is an elected leader and they do not 'deliver the goods' that leader will be attacked. Because of their dependency, group members will often go to great lengths to comply with what they suppose to be *group norms*. Others will often aid them in this process by making the rules.

Conflict – The unrealistic expectations that members hold become disillusioned by group experience. Some therapists fall into the trap of trying to be the perfect parent: they are either inexperienced or gratifying their own narcissistic needs. Lateness, absence, non-cooperation, scapegoating and aggressive criticism of other members is characteristic of this stage. Paradoxically, if this stage is passed through wholeheartedly and not avoided, trust, tenderness and a variety of expression emerges. For instance, many people avoid anger in relationships because in their past it was used as a weapon. In a group, however, they may come to understand that anger can be a relationship-building emotion, although this will only happen if the group can tolerate the initial discomfort the anger creates.

Intimacy – Little by little reality creeps into a group. The surest sign of this, as with many things, is that opposites can be allowed to exist together, thus avoiding childlike extremes. For instance the leader is neither viewed as a parental guru or a complete incompetent, but is, rather, seen as a person.

COMMON INTER-PERSONAL PHENOMENA
WITH NOURISHING OR TOXIC CONSEQUENCES

Redefining reality – Groups tend to form their own realities, especially when there is little or no reference to the outside world, as in certain kinds of intensive group therapies where there is a charismatic leader. Group members may be unaware of the intensity of the group's adjusted reality until they come to oppose it. The effect upon the individual is rather like that upon the boatman who has got used to drifting downstream with the current and decides to turn round.

Group norms – These are less to do with beliefs (as described in the previous paragraph) and more to do with what is acceptable behaviour. In the early stages of a group where security and rules are anxiously sought, *group norms* are often established which become limiting later on, both to individuals and to the progress of the group as a whole.

Rewards – Reward and punishment are devices that may get used within a group to ward off those things which it perceives as a threat. Thus a member who contravenes a norm or challenges perceived reality may be ostracized, whilst someone else might repress their true feelings in order to feel included. As we have seen, people in groups tend to repeat their early experiences and it is responses like these that a skilled *conductor* will pick up and help the group to explore. Where the group is not a therapeutic one, or where the therapy in question is not one that recognizes these and similar unconscious phenomena, severe constraint will inevitably be placed upon the overall efficacy of the group process.

Group emotions – Different from *realities* or *norms*, group emotions can sometimes be very powerful and infectious. Emotions such as sadness, joy, remorse, anger or sexual arousal can sometimes seem to fill the room. Some individuals will get caught up, frightened, defensive – or all three. In any event, such experiences enrich the group and provide material to be explored. More usually there are currents of emotion flitting about between members and within the group and, as sensitivity grows, these can be recognized and responded to openly.

Collusion – On the surface it may seem as though individuals in a group are cooperating with one another in the task of therapy. Very often there will also be a much less obvious collusion between a few or all of the group members to avoid certain areas or topics. Once again this is likely to be quite unconscious so the group – if it is to function at its best – must become more aware.

'Nourishing' and 'toxic' environments – The phenomena described above, along with many others, occur in most groups and probably always will. The capacity of such things either to nourish the life and process of the group, or to poison it, depends upon how the group integrates uncomfortable and hidden events and feelings into its functioning. Bearing this in mind, it is possible to understand why many committees, task-oriented or planning groups in general life so often get bogged down and become frustrated and ineffectual without anyone apparently meaning that they should. By contrast, a well run therapy group – of whatever theoretical persuasion – will need to have some way of constructively confronting painful or embarrassing issues and emotions when they arise.

HOW DIFFERENT THERAPIES USE GROUPS

Psychodynamic – The general middle ground of group work, accounting for most true Group Therapy, this usually takes place in a closed setting – that is, new members can not join halfway through – once a week, for about an hour and a half. A trained, non-directive *conductor* will be present who will recognize the validity of all the phenomena so far described in this section.

Analytic – Known as Group Analytic Treatment, this is an extension of psychoanalysis. Patients are seen as relating to one another in the same ways as patients in analysis relate to the analyst. Sessions are always closed, may be more than once a week, and require a qualified group analyst to 'conduct' proceedings.

Transactional Analysis – This was designed to take place in groups (as is Gestalt Therapy and Psychodrama) and increases the patient's understanding of the ways they relate to other people using such techniques as *game analysis* and *script analysis*. Transactional Analysis (TA) is best thought of as a socially educative therapy which pays less attention to the unconscious processes going on in the group than the two therapies above. TA is by far the most widely practised group therapy.

Encounter groups – TA, Person Centred Therapy and Gestalt Therapy have all, to a greater or lesser degree of success, used residential, so-called 'marathon' groups to provide therapeutic benefit. Such groups last for forty-eight hours or longer.

Setting – Groups take place in all sorts of settings; nevertheless the minimum requirements are comfort and privacy. Most therapy groups have about eight members.

Aim – The aim is to increase personal knowledge and understanding when relating to others.

Technique – It works through a mutual participation by group members, with observations and interpretations by the therapist depending upon the particular kind of group therapy.

Good points – It provides a highly adaptable setting for a variety of approaches. Although all psychotherapy can, at times, be painful, Group Therapy is often very enjoyable to be a part of. The evidence is that many people are helped to think more deeply about their lives through their experience in groups.

Often effective for – It is good for relationship difficulties, problems in groups, compulsive repetition of self-depriving behaviour, and general dissatisfaction with life. Group Therapy is the basis behind many self-help groups.

Bad points – It is possible to hide behind defences, even in well run groups.

Seldom effective for – Unlikely to be effective as a primary treatment for pronounced anxiety, phobias, addiction or crisis.

Cost – This is highly variable but usually reasonable.

Availability – Groups are ubiquitous but care should be taken to make sure that the kind of therapy you want is really what is practised: Group Therapy is a big umbrella that can shelter charlatans as well as the genuine article.

Commitment – This is high because it affects everyone else when someone does not turn up, or is late.

Training – This, of course, depends upon the kind of group it is. If possible, go through a large organization or accrediting body (*for example, see Resource Guide, under Transactional Analysis or Gestalt Therapy*).

FURTHER PSYCHOTHERAPIES FROM ADLERIAN TO SEX THERAPY

ADLERIAN THERAPY

Adlerian therapy is more properly known as **Individual Analysis**. Alfred Adler was initially a disciple of Freud but broke away to form his own theories of the human psyche and its healing. Adler emphasized the part that social influences play in shaping a person's development. He asserted that we choose goals for ourselves based upon our subjective appreciation of our world, mind, body and feelings. Adler considered humans to be innately creative and self-determinant. Three terms are important in the Individual Analytic approach:

Holistic – the notion that a person is indivisible and does not have a psyche that can be split into parts. This puts Adler in ideological opposition to, for instance, Freud and Jung.

Social – the rationale behind a person's actions can only be understood when viewed in their appropriate context. This is in opposition to the idea of a clinic or consulting room.

Teleological – a person's goals and the personal (so-called 'private') logic which guides them can be understood from their behaviour.

Individual Analysts believe that everyone is born with a desire to belong to the wider group as it is progressively experienced: family, large group, society and human race. In this theory, everyone starts off feeling 'inferior', but by maturity will have worked their way to a position of mutuality within the various groups. Mentally healthy individuals are perceived as being confident of their place in, and their contribution to, the groups to which they belong. To this end there are three life tasks which occupy the person: work, friendship and love.

In the Adlerian view of the psyche, problems occur when feelings of inferiority persist and are compensated for by a striving for personal superiority. Those who feel *less than* others and have to behave as if they are superior deprive themselves of the opportunity to succeed in work, friendship and love, or long-term partnership. Such people are preoccupied with triumphing over others and cannot make a mutual contribution within the groups to which they are attached.

Inevitably, conflicts develop between the individual's experience – of failure – and their internal belief – of superiority, and they have to develop a reasoning that justifies the pointlessness of much of their behaviour. An example would be someone thinking: 'I could easily be top in my class but the teaching is bad', in order to preserve the person from facing the truth that they are, on average, equal to others.

A child's failure to develop and mature beyond appropriate feelings of inferiority are usually due to early experiences. Examples are:

Overprotection – Which spoils the child's capacity for accomplishment because they have not learnt the personal pleasure of struggling to achieve a goal.

Criticism – Which engenders a fear in the child of taking risks
and possibly making mistakes. Thus they do not even try,
and feel doubly inferior as a consequence.

Competition – An overly competitive environment is one where
discouragement prevails. Siblings, instead of being supportive, undermine each other for fear that there is not
enough 'feeling of belonging' to go round.

THE THERAPEUTIC APPROACH

Therapy involves four factors:

Building a therapeutic relationship – In which a sense of
mutuality and honesty between the therapist and the client
is paramount.

Exploration – Of the early life, attitudes and goals of the
patient. The therapist gains information on those aspects
that the patient is unaware of, such as hidden motives and
desires, from the way in which the patient presents himself
and what he does not say.

Interpretation and insight – Conflicting goals and consequent
self-justifying reasoning are presented to the client in progressive steps for comparison and discussion. This is a
skilled process because the patient may very easily feel persecuted by the therapist.

Reorientation – Where new patterns of behaviour will be experimented with. Initially this takes place between the therapist and patient, but soon it starts to involve the patient with
their 'living groups' in the absence of the therapist.

SEX THERAPY

Since the pioneering work of the American research team of Masters and Johnson in the 1960s and 70s, **Sex Therapy** has become an important branch of Behavioural Therapy. As fewer individuals and couples feel forced to suffer in silence, the demand for help with such problems as erectile impotence (difficulty achieving or maintaining an erection), premature or delayed ejaculation, male or female inability to achieve orgasm, and pain during intercourse has increased.

The aim of Sex Therapy is to help an individual or couple to improve the quality of their sex life or relationships and to help an acceptance of sexuality.

THE THERAPEUTIC APPROACH

As with any behavioural therapy:

The problem is carefully investigated with the individual or couple, and treatment goals are set.

Tasks are set for 'homework' and are attempted before the next meeting with the therapist.

The results of the attempts are discussed and any factors making them difficult explored, so that further understanding of the problems and a means of remedy can be arrived at.

Modified or enhanced tasks are attempted between sessions and feedback continues.

Emphasis is thus placed upon the patient's capacity to take responsibility for change.

A couple attend a clinic because the female partner finds penetration painful and cannot achieve orgasm. Her partner finds it hard to stop after a certain point. He feels guilty, she avoids sex; they both feel guilty.

The *behavioural* component of the treatment involves progressive steps, from practising talking about what each other finds pleasurable and unsatisfactory or difficult, to simple touching of each other (except for genitalia), then progressing to genital contact and then to intercourse, with progressive degrees of penetration and thrusting. The aim is for each partner to be confident about the wellbeing of the other, as well as deriving satisfaction for themselves. A behavioural device that is often used in this process is that the couple practise stopping at certain points during intercourse. This enhances a feeling of security and reduces the fear of one partner being hurt or hurting the other.

In tandem with the behavioural treatment, the skilled therapist will use psychotherapeutic and counselling skills to help investigate any misunderstandings and any negative attitudes to the sexual act, to giving and receiving pleasure, and to the therapy itself. In this way, and by incorporating educational components, the couple or individual is equipped to solve other problems that may occur either between themselves or with subsequent partners.

PRIMAL THERAPY

Primal Therapy was developed during the 1960s by Arthur Janov. While practising group therapy, Janov asked a patient to cry out for his mother and father to see what result this had. The patient became increasingly distressed and emotional, and began twitching and shaking. Shortly thereafter he gave vent to

a sobbing scream of agony and relief. Afterwards the patient felt that he could feel his feelings in a way that he never had before. Janov developed techniques for helping patients to utter their *primal scream*, which was then followed by insights and emotional growth.

From his observations, Janov developed a theory of neurosis that centred around a failure to satisfy the basic needs of the infant.

Firstly, the early environment fails to gratify the infant's needs adequately.

The child realizes that its needs for love and acceptance will never be met.

This realization is utterly traumatic and becomes the bedrock of the disordered adult personality.

The real self is repressed (because it is believed to be unwanted) and the facade is created (because it is believed to be what is wanted by others and therefore likely to generate love and acceptance).

Psychological and physiological pressure builds up in the person causing the neurotic pain of day to day existence.

THE THERAPEUTIC APPROACH

Primal therapy helps the individual revisit the beginning of their lives before, or at, the point when the real self is repressed – hence the agony and also the relief.

Just like birth, the therapy itself is dramatic and, in its way, violent. The aim is to break down the defences in one go (as opposed to the piecemeal way in which many other therapies nibble at them). At the centre of the sessions – which usually take place in groups – is the *primal*, in which by a process of suggestion and encouragement the patient apparently re-experiences their birth. The therapist conducts the proceedings, encouraging the individual to breathe in certain ways and cry out, while other members of the group gather round with pillows and cushions to push in on the individual, like walls of the womb. The actual *primal* is a totally engulfing experience in which the patient becomes foetal in their posture and movements and makes sounds like a baby.

Following these dam-breaking experiences, the quieter and calmer aspects of the therapy continue in the group setting and individuals explore their experiences together and learn about their true feelings.

The ultimate goal of the therapy is for the patient to be less dominated by their unmet needs and thus more able to find out how they really feel and what they really want to do.

MARITAL OR COUPLE THERAPY

Couple Therapy is a postwar phenomenon which has grown as people have come to understand that relationships can be improved with skilled outside help. Couple therapy either takes place in the setting of a mental health clinic, when the emotional wellbeing of one or both partners is thought to be affected, or in community settings with organizations like *Relate*, (which used to be *Marriage Guidance Counselling*). All couple therapies, whatever their theoretical standpoint, make the assumption that both the problems and the source of the remedy lie in the relationship between the pair. Marital therapy recognizes three life cycle stages through which a typical couple pass and in which they may experience different types of problem:

Early stage – The capacity for physical and emotional exploration and adjustment is required for daily living and the

setting of long-term goals. Problems arise when one or both of the couple has difficulty disengaging from parents, or feels disappointment when confronted with the reality of living together, or when small children disrupt the dynamics of the couple's relationship.

Middle stage – There is normally a period of stability when a couple know each other well and their children become more self-sufficient. Difficulties become apparent when boredom, a sense of lack of achievement and parental loss overwhelm a couple's capacity to adjust and to be mutually supportive. Dissatisfaction may result in clandestine relationships which further undermine the couple's unity.

Late stage – Eventually couples face the absence of their children and have to adjust to being on their own together – something that they may have managed to avoid for years. Ill health and old age are more common at this stage, and these add stress to relationships.

TYPES OF COUPLE THERAPY

Psychodynamic – Drawing on a psychoanalytic understanding of unconscious motivation and expectation, the therapist uses their interpretations to help the couple become more aware of buried and avoided realities. The analytic process is often quite painful because of the uncomfortable nature of what is exposed. The underlying belief is that each person's early experiences and hidden conflicts are being played out in the relationship in destructive ways. For instance, a man might unwittingly attempt to make his partner conform to the ingrained, dysfunctional ways of relating that he resorted to with the mother he loved, but who disappointed him. Try as she might, his wife will always feel inadequate and unable to fulfil herself in the relationship: she can never make up for the things that are lacking in her partner – and she even feels that they are lacking in herself.

Transactional – Rules, assumptions, decision making and methods of communication between the couple are explored with the therapist or therapists. The aim of therapy is to help the partners see the ways in which they restrict, manipulate and undermine each other even when their intention may be quite the opposite. Specific examples are taken from the couple's everyday life and examined in exhaustive detail, the hope being that once revealed, bad habits are very difficult to slip back into and the couple can now find new and more balanced ways of operating.

Behavioural – Using learning theory, (*see Behaviour Psychotherapy*) the therapist helps the couple to identify ways in which aspects of behaviour or attitudes that each finds undesirable in the other are unwittingly encouraged and reinforced in their lives together. Partners are required to suggest alternative behaviours and the rewards that will follow if these are put into effect. Although this sounds a very mechanical and clinical 'give to get' approach to improving a couples' relationship, the focus that it produces upon their behaviour has proved beneficial. For instance, a particular problem might be that when the working partner returns home they seem to ignore the other. By looking very closely at the assumptions that each makes, and by agreeing to spend time talking about the day when they meet up in the evening, communication begins to replace misunderstanding, nagging and resentment.

FAMILY THERAPY

Family Therapy usually takes place following the referral of a child or adolescent member to a specialist unit. Family therapy has evolved over the last few decades into a set of theoretical approaches which, although different in emphasis (*see below*), see the child not simply as 'the problem', but rather as part of a family system in which a difficulty of behaviour or emotion has arisen.

For the initial assessment, all those living at home – both parents and siblings – will be asked to attend. One or more therapists will be present at this and subsequent interviews, which will be aimed at defining the problems as they affect the family, and working out ways in which these can be alleviated.

APPROACHES TO FAMILY THERAPY

Psychodynamic – In an extension of Psychoanalytic theory and method, family problems are seen as originating in the past experiences of all the members of the family and the upbringing of the parent or parents. Just as in analysis, the therapist helps the family to see the links between past experience and present behaviour in creating and perpetuating their problems. The therapist lets the family know what it is like to be with them and offers insights into what may be going on that they are not aware of. Slowly the myths, misunderstandings and selfishness within the family are exposed, and responsibility for them is taken.

Systematic/Communicative – Unrecognized and unacknowledged ways of communicating and setting rules are explored. Mixed messages and distorted interactions are looked at and understood for what they do to the self-esteem and wellbeing of family members. Therapists adopt different approaches depending upon whether they see themselves primarily as teaching the family to make good rules and to communicate well, or as facilitating the family's capacity to modify and improve its ways of communicating in a way unique to the individuals involved.

Behavioural – Each member of the family (not just the individual labelled as 'the problem') exhibits behaviour which is reinforced (*see Behavioural Therapy*) by the behaviour of the others. Not only is undesirable behaviour unwittingly reinforced but desirable behaviour is rarely rewarded. The therapist seeks to help the family understand the behaviours and then encourage them to make more appropriate and easily monitored *behavioural contracts* with one another.

Role-play – This is often an adjunct to other forms of therapy and involves the replay of a familiar family scene so that the family and therapist can discuss what is going on and try to find alternatives.

CLINICAL EXAMPLE

John is twelve, he has been referred for Family Therapy because of problems at home and school. John has an eight year-old sister. His father has been looking after both of them since his mother left the family two years ago, at which time he and his sister were close playmates. Six months ago, all three moved in with Shona and her two children. John's school has complained that John has been bullying and not working well and at home he seems to delight in deliberately upsetting everyone else.

The assessment revealed that John's sister was now spending her time with her stepsister, and that John was getting much less time on his own with his father. His bad behaviour erupted because he felt envious of others when they were having a good time and felt driven to spoil it. Because of this he got a bad

name at school and at home for being difficult and a trouble-
maker and began to be left out of things. Fearful that he was no
longer wanted, he resorted to getting the attention he needed by
further disruption and naughtiness.

Therapy involved helping his parents to see his behaviour as
a cry for help and in adjustments being made to the way the
family thought about him, so that he could feel safe and wanted
again.

CHILD PSYCHOTHERAPY

Occasionally it will be thought necessary for a child to be seen
individually as well as, or instead of, in a family or group. Very
often the child will have difficulties with his or her emotions
and demonstrate it through behaviour which is unconsciously
designed to alert their carers to their plight. The principal
examples are:

> not eating
>
> underachieving at school
>
> being ill
>
> being uncharacteristically naughty

The repetition of *maladaptive* behaviour – such as constantly
stealing even when it results in punishment and withdrawal of
privilege – and symptoms such as aggression or sadness, result
from inner conflicts. Examples of these conflicts are:

> The conflict between what seems available and what is
> longed for – for example, withdrawn or distracted parent-
> ing versus the child's desire for affection and security.

The conflict between what seems to be expected and what seems right – for example, self-sufficiency versus the child's need for nurture.

THE THERAPEUTIC APPROACH

The aim is to:

Create a secure, permissive and non-critical relationship with the child through warmth, respect and being non-judgmental.

Help the child to find ways of expressing his or her inner thoughts and feelings. This may need to be symbolic, through play, rather than by simply talking together.

Reach a better understanding of the child's inner world – what it is like to be the child – and reflect this back to them.

Help the child to reintegrate into the family and school.

There are many different approaches to child therapy. Some place more emphasis upon play whilst others place it upon knowledge of child development. Realistically, a good child therapist will be someone who is able to enter the child's world unselfconsciously, whilst at the same time being able to draw on a wide resource of experience and training. A pragmatic approach is necessary when working with children because of the tendency that children have to inspire extreme reactions, such as pity, anger or hopelessness, in their therapists. Often environmental changes can be made within the family, such as the child spending more time with one or other parent, or moving to a room of their own, or the therapist teaching the parents to make and determinedly stick to rules. At other times helping school teachers to understand a particular child's difficulties more clearly or moving a child away from bullies is all the intervention that is required. This aspect of child psychotherapy means that it is rarely practicable outside the environment of a clinic that is fully integrated into the social and medical services of the community.

PERSONAL CONSTRUCT THERAPY

This is a very complex theory developed in the USA by George Kelly. **Personal Construct Therapy**, or PCT, has elements of Existential Therapy and of behavioural theory. It is based upon the idea that people see the world through *constructs* or 'mental spectacles' which, in effect, colour their perception of the surrounding world. Kelly argued that it was not possible to take these spectacles off, but it was possible to change the lenses to ones that are more helpful. The therapist and client work together to discover what the individual's problematic or self-defeating *constructs* are, and then set about changing them. There are many different ways to do this; they include writing, role-play, talking and use of dreams. Although PCT need not be a long therapy, it should not be entered into lightly.

NEURO-LINGUISTIC PROGRAMMING

On the fringes of true psychotherapy, **NLP** borrows many aspects of other therapies and relies upon the capacity of the individual to alter their view of various troubling aspects of life by way of appropriate mental exercises. Some exercises are motivational whilst others involve hypnosis or self-hypnosis.

HYPNOTHERAPY

Hypnotherapy is not really a psychotherapy but is often linked with it in people's minds. One reason for this might be that early psychoanalysts, such as Sigmund Freud, used hypnosis to gain access to unconscious thoughts, but later decided that dreams and *free associating* (saying whatever comes into your mind) were more effective. There is too much abdication of personal responsibility on the part of the patient for Hypnotherapy to fulfil the criteria for a psychotherapy that I outlined at the beginning of the book.

FEMINIST PSYCHOTHERAPY

Although strictly speaking there is no such thing as Feminist Psychotherapy, as an orientation within many of the different therapies it is very important. The common factor is a particular social or political perspective. One effect this has is to repudiate the power differences that sometimes exist between therapists and their clients as being a reflection of male-oriented hierarchical systems in society. Feminist-oriented therapists generally see men as well as women, and should be considered as an option if being fully involved in decision making about therapy is particularly important to you.

ENCOUNTER GROUPS

Encounter Groups were an important part of the Human Potential Movement *(see page 5)* but are much less common now than they used to be. Encounter Groups last for a day or a weekend. They rely upon the intensiveness of the experience to erode peoples' social defence; thus the group as a whole can support each other as they find out what they are really like by interacting in a

110   safe but unavoidable group. All Encounter Groups have a *facilitator* or *conductor* and it tends to be this person who sets the tone of the group. Some groups are very emotional and confrontational and others are more gentle. Meeting the facilitator is a sensible precaution before committing oneself to an Encounter Group.

CO-COUNSELLING

What makes **Co-Counselling** stand out from other therapies is its high degree of mutuality. After an initial training in counselling techniques, people pair up with one another and meet at mutually convenient times to take it in turn to be therapist and client. Co-Counselling is a very liberal form of therapy which celebrates the authenticity of emotional expression. By its very nature, Co-Counselling blurs the boundaries between everyday life and therapy especially if, for instance, counsellors happen to be flatmates. For this reason Co-Counselling can become rather a way of life for some people.

TRANSPERSONAL PSYCHOLOGY

Transpersonal Psychology is limited in availability; it combines aspects of personal spirituality with conventional ideas on how early experiences lead people to be defensive in adulthood. Transpersonal Psychologists work with imagery, dreams, daydreams, meditation, writing, drawing, painting and guided fantasies.

Very noisy and cathartic, **Bioenergetics** relies not on words but actions. By using various kinds of movement, touching and breathing exercises, therapists help people to release pent-up emotions and blocked feelings so that they begin to feel better about themselves. This therapy and similar *action therapies* are undoubtedly very exciting and cathartic to take part in, although there is always the risk that catharsis will be mistaken for psychological growth. The real test is whether or not any apparent changes are long lasting.

4

GETTING STARTED

FINDING A GOOD PSYCHOTHERAPIST –
WHAT TO LOOK FOR AT THE FIRST INTERVIEW

Having got to this point, the reader should be in a good position to decide which kind of therapy best suits their needs, pocket and temperament. The next step is to make contact with a therapist who has been recommended by a friend or organization and to arrange a meeting. This is usually done on the telephone but some people prefer to write. Sometimes this process is made easier by the therapy centre or organization which, for example, may have advertised a course to which you have responded, and who will invite you for an interview. There are general considerations to be made, on the side of the therapist as well as the patient, that are important when it comes to deciding whether or not to agree to work together, either in a one-to-one fashion or in a group.

CHARACTERISTICS OF
A 'GOOD ENOUGH' THERAPIST

Genuine – It is a bad sign if the therapist seems to be putting on a show. This is different from being professional, which requires the therapist to hold aspects of their personality in the background. A therapist who does not seem to be 'being themselves' with spontaneity and ease should be avoided.

Respectful – For many people their prospective psychotherapist will be the first stranger in whom they have confided so much. For this reason it is important that the therapist is understanding, openly receptive and unshockable. If your therapist begins the relationship by confusing you with their own strong reactions to your story then they are best avoided.

Encouraging – It is important that your therapist is able to be positive and encouraging. An atmosphere of realistic optimism is an indication that they have seen much worse and will help you feel that, with appropriate input from you, a difference can be made to your life.

Understandable – The therapist will outline what he or she sees as the aim of the interview clearly and understandably. Make sure you know in advance how long you have to talk together and whether there can be more than one interview. This all helps to reduce anxiety and help you keep a clear head in what might be emotional or upsetting times. During the interview it is important that you ask the therapist to explain anything you do not understand. The way the therapist responds to such questions will be a good guide to their competence.

Sensitive – Expect your therapist to be alert and sensitive to you as an individual. If you feel that you are having to adjust to them more than they are adjusting to you it may be that they are over-rigid or uninvolved. It is quite normal to feel a little intimidated and in need of guidance and support on first contact with a psychotherapy and its practitioner. A competent therapist will be able to put a prospective patient at their ease and behave in a way that minimizes the intimidating nature of the process. The best guide of someone's general level of 'responsive sensitivity' is the language they use. A competent therapist will notice if something he or she says jars on or confuses you, and will adjust accordingly in order to aid communication. You should regard the failure to do this as serious, as it may mean that the therapist is not paying enough attention to the 'reality' of you.

Practical – If the therapist agrees to see you or involve you in a group there will most likely be practical considerations such as timing and money to sort out. It is important that these things can be discussed and dealt with early on, so that the therapy is not disrupted by chaotic arrangements or inflexibility on the part of either party. It is worth noting at this point that the therapy starts on the very first contact. The way in which the patient and the therapist work together from the very beginning is a good indication of how well they will work together later.

Interested – In your past as well as the present. Most of the effective psychotherapies rely to some extent upon an understanding of how past events, particularly in early childhood, have come to affect the present. Be prepared to remember what you can and appreciate the therapist who takes time and trouble to ask you directly about your past instead of making professional, and possibly inaccurate, assumptions based upon what you are like today.

Relaxed and in control – This is really another way of saying that the therapist should seem competent and trustworthy. They should not be overbearing, at a loss, or anxious about the meeting. The best indicator that the therapist is relaxed and appropriately confident is if some of the same feelings begin to grow in the patient during the interview.

Confidential – Confidentiality is a major issue and quite rightly so. Make sure that you know how confidential your sessions will be, especially in a group setting or if the therapist is a trainee and therefore has a supervisor.

Able to finish the interview – This may seem an odd point but endings are hard when there is emotional material around. Very often, during therapy of any kind, issues of beginning and ending will emerge. How punctual and well-managed were the beginnings and endings of your first encounter with the therapist? And, perhaps just as interestingly, were you on time and did you try to make the interview go on longer than agreed?

Our aim here is not to be critical of therapists but rather to increase the confidence of anyone thinking of becoming involved in psychotherapy. After all, the hardest and most important step anyone makes in therapy is the first phone call.

FREQUENTLY ASKED QUESTIONS

What is the difference between a psychotherapist, a psychiatrist, a psychologist and a psychoanalyst?
A psychiatrist is someone who has trained as a medical doctor and then specialized in mental illness. There are sub-specialities

of psychiatry such as *child psychiatry*, *psychiatry of old age*, *forensic psychiatry* and *psychotherapy*. This does not mean that all psychotherapists are psychiatrists – far from it – but some are. Psychotherapists are drawn from every conceivable background, from the arts to medicine, but very often they tend to be people who have begun their careers in some kind of caring role. Psychoanalysts are all, by definition, psychotherapists, but very few psychotherapists are psychoanalysts. A high proportion of psychoanalysts are psychiatrists but very few psychiatrists are psychoanalysts. I hope that's clear!

A psychologist is someone who has been to university and studied for a degree in psychology. From there the possibilities are diverse and lead into education, industry, mental health and therapy.

How do I get therapy on the NHS?
By arranging to be referred by your family doctor to the psychotherapy unit of the local psychiatric hospital. This need not be as daunting as it might sound because most psychotherapy units are housed separately in their own building. Many kinds of psychotherapy are available through the NHS, but on a rather ad hoc basis. What is available will depend upon where you live.

Which therapies use the couch and what is the point?
Freud (*see Psychoanalysis*) developed the use of the couch whereby the patient lies down and the analyst sits behind their head, out of view but close by. This is a familiar image in cartoons; however only Psychoanalysts, Psychoanalytic Psychotherapists and some Jungians use the technique. Despite its rather comical or frightening associations, the couch is found to be extremely useful:

The patient can neither see the therapist nor 'read' their body language and facial expressions. This leaves the therapist in a much better position to be mistaken for important people in the patient's past.

When lying down the body is more relaxed than sitting up and, so it is thought, the mind is more able to wander and *free associate*, as the analysts put it. This effect is further enhanced by the fact that it is hard to stare around the room and visually distract oneself whilst lying down.

Another form of distraction which is reduced by lying down is that of muscular activity. The result of all these factors is that many of the thoughts that would ordinarily go unnoticed in everyday life are a little more obvious during the therapy session.

What if I am attracted to my therapist or my therapist is attracted to me?
This is much more common than people realize and is perfectly normal and understandable. What is less common than those who seek to attack psychotherapy would like to believe is the therapist or patient taking advantage of the situation and sabotaging the therapy. There are a number of reasons why a patient may feel attracted to their therapist:

Simply, they are attractive.

They mistake them for someone else that they desire or have desired in the past.

They find it hard to tell the difference between the intimacy associated with caring and being in love.

They secretly want to sabotage the therapy or gain power over the therapist.

A mixture of the above.

Interestingly, the reasons why a therapist might be attracted to a patient are exactly the same. If the therapy and therapist are any good these feelings will be looked at in the cool light of day and used in the therapeutic process. The general rule is that if you are sexually attracted to your therapist you should say so.

What can I do if my therapy is not working?
It is nearly always a bad sign if you do not feel this at some stage of the treatment. However badly someone may want to get things sorted out, there will always be a part of them that resists change. After all, change whether it is good or bad can be frightening. Therapeutic growth can also mean giving up cosy grievances, facing uncomfortable truths about oneself, and feeling pain where previously there was numbness. The resistant part of the patient kicks back and one of the commonest ways is to attack the therapy or therapist as being no good. Put briefly, if the patient is not resisting then the therapist is not 'therapising'.

Is psychotherapy useful for schizophrenia?
Not on its own. There have been many attempts to treat *psychotic illness* (schizophrenia is a psychotic illness) with psychotherapy, but most people agree that schizophrenia and other very serious mental illnesses, such as suicidal depression or mania, are best treated with drugs and then backed up by therapy when the person is able to think clearly again and reflect on their situation with someone else.

Yes of course they will. Many counsellors will be happy to see
you but there are specific places you can go to, such as the
Brook Advisory Centre or the British Pregnancy Advisory Service *(see Resource Guide for details)*. Both these organizations will
be able to guide you to local help. Difficulties after having a termination are now so widely acknowledged that your doctor
will probably suggest that you arrange counselling in advance.

**What therapy is available for people with AIDS or someone
caring for an AIDS sufferer?**
This is changing and improving all the time. Contact the
National AIDS help line *(see Resource Guide for details)*.

**I have recently been bereaved and need to talk about it. Is
there somewhere I can go?**
For bereavement in general, Cruse are excellent. For cot death
and still birth contact the Stillbirth and Neonatal Death Society
(see Resource Guide for details).

**I am unhappy at work but do not know if it is me or the job.
Where can I get help?**
A good place to contact for general or local advice is the
Employee Advisory Resource *(see Resource Guide for details)*.

**I think someone in my house is being sexually abused. Is
there someone I can talk to in confidence?**
You should contact the NSPCC *(see Resource Guide for details)*.

I would like to have therapy from someone from my own cultural background. Where can I get advice?

Psychotherapy from someone of your own ethnic or cultural background is likely to be something that will need searching out locally. Nevertheless, wherever you live a good start would be The Inter-Cultural Therapy Centre (*see Resource Guide for details*).

I am gay and want to be seen by a gay therapist. How do I go about this?

Think twice about ruling out a psychotherapist because of their heterosexual agenda. Providing they are not hostile or prejudiced, or lack understanding, it is the quality of the therapist that should be your primary aim, not their orientation. Having said this, for certain issues a gay therapist might be the most suitable. The London Lesbian and Gay Switchboard are the best informed (*see Resource Guide for details*).

What about clergy who are in emotional difficulties?

It is quite common for those who are in a pastoral or care-giving role to have difficulties of their own which eventually surface. Clergy will meet an informed and sympathetic reception at the Dympna Centre (*see Resource Guide for details*).

Should I haggle with my therapist about fees?

Yes and no. If you want to see a therapist but can not afford his or her fees, then say so and see if there is a reduction available: it will not be much but it might make all the difference. Some charitable organizations that offer therapy operate a sliding scale that is based upon the patient's earnings: you pay what you earn in an hour. Negotiating the fee only becomes a problem when it enters the therapy as an issue, so once an agreement has been made it should be stuck to.

In my opinion, it is not a sign of psychological health to dedicate one's life to helping others. Nevertheless many people, whether they realize it or not, enter the world of psychotherapy with this sort of aim in mind. Usually they are responding to something from their past. For instance, if they feel that they were not cared for and listened to when young, they may have an unconscious desire to 'do a better job' for others and so try to ameliorate their own disappointment. Perhaps they are so afraid of their own neediness that they are driven to the extreme of seeing it in others – thinking 'neediness is someone else's problem, not mine' – and treating them for it. None of this matters if the training that the would-be therapist receives is one that explores these areas and reveals the truth behind their motivation. For this reason, therapists who have had intensive therapy of their own are the only ones to take seriously. Good therapists are not perfect, sorted out people; they are people who have sorted out how imperfect they are.

What does the word 'subconscious' mean?
Nothing as far as psychotherapy is concerned. It is used by people when they mean the *unconscious*. The unconscious is that part of our feelings and motivations that we are unaware of and that we cannot become aware of by trying to remember. Things that we know but can not remember have, as everyone knows, been forgotten, and reside in the *pre-conscious* waiting to be remembered.

I am in group therapy and there is someone in it I want to go out with. What should we do?
The really clever thing to do is talk about it in the group because the attraction has arisen in the group and may have something to do with others. There is a wider principle here: that is the

problems that arise when sub-groups of a bigger group get together in the pub and talk about the others – not a good idea. If you are attracted to someone or just want to be friends, try to wait until the group is over. You may feel differently then anyway.

I can not remember much about my childhood. Does this matter if I am thinking of having psychotherapy?

No. Repressed memories from childhood return when it is safe enough for them to do so. Important feelings and events will surface during your therapy and there is no point in trying to force them, or rely on what others tell you about your past. It is what you remember and you feel that is important.

Will psychotherapy destroy my creativity?

No, but it might alter the motivation that you have for being creative and the way that you express it. It is much more likely that therapy will release greater and more genuine creativity, especially if you are able to explore the destructive urges that are essential to true creativity, but often mistakenly repressed.

My therapist is a member of several organizations that sound very impressive. What does this tell me about him or her?

Nothing. Make a note of your prospective therapist's affiliations and memberships and contact the bodies concerned to see what criteria they set for association. In some cases you will find that your therapist has been through a rigorous training and in other cases that they have merely sent someone some money. Remember, anyone can call themselves a psychotherapist and start practising 'psychotherapy'.

It is very common to begin by liking one's psychotherapist and then, at some point in the therapy, to begin to dislike them. Feelings of persecution, distrust and incompatibility can surface seemingly from nowhere. Invariably these feelings are associated with someone other than the therapist: they might be feelings we have about someone in our past, or even about ourselves. The important thing to remember is that they may well have been suppressed for a long time and so feel like new thoughts, when in fact they are very old and have been covertly informing our attitude to others all our lives. Feelings of dislike towards the therapist should always be shared with them; only in this way can they be properly understood.

I feel disloyal talking about my family 'behind their backs'. There does not seem to be any point in pointing the finger of blame after all these years.
It is a common misconception of psychotherapy that it seeks to find someone to 'blame' for the condition that a patient finds him or herself in. Paradoxically, the very reason that people seek help is often because they cannot stop nursing their grievances and take responsibility for themselves. Facts are facts and they have to be talked about in order to find out the truth. I usually find that when a patient is reluctant to examine the true role of others in their difficulties it is because they are afraid of undermining a cosy grievance that gives them permission to be demanding of, or inconsiderate towards, others.

What if I go to pieces during therapy and can not pull myself together again?
This is one way of voicing a fear that many people have when they consider the option of psychotherapy. The fear is of going mad. Anyone who is organized enough to get help from a

psychotherapist and commit themselves to turning up will find sufficient reserves of personal strength to survive and develop through the process. Feeling as if you are going to pieces and actually going mad are two very different things.

What if my therapist tells me to do something I do not want to do?
Do not do it, but be prepared to talk about why not.

I would rather talk to someone I know, I think I would find it easier than telling a stranger.
Sometimes it is hard for people to decide whether they are looking for a therapist or a friend. It is precisely because they are strangers that a therapist can be someone with whom you have a new and unusual relationship: once your work is over you can walk away from each other. In any case, friends have a habit of telling us what we want to hear or what they think we want to hear, not what we need to hear.

RESOURCE GUIDE

More idea of what is obtainable from the various therapies is available from:

GREAT BRITAIN

Psychoanalysis:
London Centre for Psychotherapy
19 Fitzjohns Avenue
London NW3 5JY

British Association for Psychotherapy
121 Hendon Lane
London NW3 3PR

The British Psychoanalytic Society
63 New Cavendish Street
London W1M 7RD
0171 580 4952

Psychoanalytic Psychotherapy:
Institute of Psychoanalysis
63 New Cavendish Street
London W1M 7RD

British Association for Psychotherapy
121 Hendon Lane
London NW3 3PR

Scottish Institute of Human Relations
56 Albany Street
Edinburgh EH1 3QR
0131 556 0924

Tavistock Clinic
120 Belsize Lane
London NW3 5BA

Analytical Psychology:
Society of Analytical Psychology
1 Daleham Gardens
London NW3 3BY

Association of Jungian Analysts
Flat 3
7 Eton Avenue
London NW3 3EL

Existential Therapy:
Society for Existential Analysis
Psychology Department
Regent's College
Inner Circle
Regent's Park
London NW1 4NS

Behavioural Therapy:
British Association of Behavioural Psychotherapy
7 Whittaker Street
Radcliffe
Manchester M26 9TD
0161 724 6321

Psychological Treatment Unit
Maudsley Hospital
London SE5 8AZ
0171 703 6333

Cognitive Therapy:
Institute of Psychiatry
De Crespigny Park
London SE5 8AF

Person Centred Therapy:
The Association of Humanistic Psychology
62 Southwark Bridge Road
London SE1
0345 660326

British Association for Counselling
37a Sheep Street
Rugby
Warwickshire CV21 3BX

Norwich Centre for Personal and Professional Development
7 Earlham Road
Norwich NR2 3RA

Transactional Analysis:
More information on local resources can be obtained from:

Institute of Transactional Analysis
BM Box 4104
London WC1 3XX

Gestalt Therapy:
The Gestalt Centre, London
64 Warwick Road
St Albans
Hertfordshire AL1 4DL

The Gestalt Psychotherapy Training Institute UK
P.O. Box 620
Bristol BS99 7DL

Psychodrama:
British Psychodrama Association
2a Kingsway
Wembley
Middlesex HA9 7QR

Morpeth Centre for Psychotherapy
40 Grosvenor Place
Jesmond
Newcastle-on-Tyne NE2 2RE
0191 281 6243

Holwell Centre for Psychodrama
East Down
Barnstaple
Devon EX31 4NZ
01271 50597

Group Therapy:
Institute for Group Analysis
1 Bickenhall Mansions
Bickenhall Street
London W1

Adlerian Therapy:
The Adlerian Society for Individual Psychology
161 Charlton Church Lane
London SE7 7AA

Sex Therapy:
Association of Sexual and Marital Therapists
PO Box 62
Sheffield S10 3TS

Primal Therapy:
London Association of Primal Psychotherapists
18a Laurier Road
London NW5 1SH

Marital or Couple Therapy:
Relate (National Marriage Guidance Council)
Herbert Gray College
Little Church Street
Rugby
Warwickshire CV21 3AP

Family Therapy:
Institute of Family Therapy
43 New Cavendish Street
London W1M 7RG

Personal Construct Therapy:
Centre for Personal Construct Psychology
132 Warwick Way
London SW1V 4JD
0171 834 8875

Neuro-Linguistic Programming:
Association for Neuro-Linguistic Programming
100b Carysfort Road
London N16 9AP
0171 241 3664

Hypnotherapy:
National Register of Hypnotherapists and Psychotherapists
12 Cross Street
Nelson
Lancashire BB9 7EN
01282 699378

Feminist Psychotherapy:
Birmingham Women's Counselling and Therapy Centre
43 Ladywood Middleway
Birmingham B16 8HA
0121 455 8677

Woman's Counselling and Therapy Service
Oxford Chambers
Oxford Place
Leeds LS1 3AX
01532 455725

Women's Therapy Centre
6 Manor Gardens
London N7 6LA
0171 263 6200

Encounter Groups:
Open Centre
188 Old Street
London EC1
0181 549 9583

Co-Counselling:
Co-Counselling Phoenix
5 Victoria Road
Sheffield S10 2DJ
01742 686371

Transpersonal Psychology:
Centre for Transpersonal Psychology
7 Pembridge Place
London W2 4XB

Bioenergetics:
British Institute of Bioenergetic Analysis
22 Fitzjohns Avenue
London NW3 5NB
0171 435 1079

Pregnancy Advice:
Brook Advisory Centre
153a East Street
London SE17 2SD
0171 708 1234

British Pregnancy Advisory Service
Austy Manor
Wootton Wawen
Solihull B95 6BX
0156 793225

AIDS Counselling:
National AIDS Help Line
PO Box 1577
Camden Town
London NW1 1DW
0800 567123

Bereavement Counselling:
Cruse House
126 Sheen Road
Richmond
London TW9 1UR
0181 940 4818

Still Birth or Cot Death Counselling:
Stillbirth and Neonatal Death Society
28 Portland Place
London W1N 4DE
0171 436 5881

Problems at work:
Employee Advisory Resource
Brunel Science Park
Kingston Lane
Uxbridge UB8 3PQ
01895 71135

Child Abuse:
NSPCC
67 Saffron Hill
London EC1N 8RS
0171 242 1626

Inter-Cultural Therapy:
The Inter-Cultural Therapy Centre
278 Seven Sisters Road
Finsbury Park
London N4 2HY
0171 263 4130

Lesbian and Gay:
The London Lesbian and Gay Switchboard
0171 837 7324

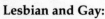

Dympna Centre
60 Grove End Road
London NW8 9NH
0171 286 6107

INTERNATIONAL

The following can be used as an initial point of contact; they
may be able to guide you to more specific therapies:

American Psychoanalytic Association
309 East 49th Street
New York
New York 10017
(212) 752 0450

Association for the Advancement of Gestalt Therapy
11611 North Meridian Street
Suite 250
Carmel
IN 46032
(317) 571 7821

American Psychological Association
750 First Street
North East
Washington DC
20002-4242

Canadian Psychological Association
Suite 205
151 Slater Street
Ottawa
Ontario
KIP 5H3
(613) 237 2144

Australian Psychological Society
1 Grattan Street
Carlton
Victoria 3053
(61 3) 9663 6166

FURTHER READING

This bibliography is a little idiosyncratic and so requires explanation. There are references which very obviously take as their subject various aspects of psychotherapy and there are some that don't. The aim is to provide thought provoking material pertaining directly or indirectly to psychotherapy and from which the inquisitive reader may launch themselves in whatever direction they like.

Apuleius, *The Golden Ass*, Penguin Classics, 1969
Bettelheim, B., *The Uses of Enchantment*, Penguin, 1976
Bunyan, J., *The Pilgrim's Progress*, Penguin, 1977
Casement, P., *On Learning from The Patient*, Routledge, 1986
Chesterton, G. K., *St. Francis of Assisi*, Hodder & Stoughton, 1964
Dryden, W., *Individual Therapy*, Open University Press, 1990
Durrell, L., *The Alexandria Quartet*, Faber & Faber, 1968
Eliot, T. S., *Collected Poems 1909–1962*, Faber & Faber, 1963

Fairbairn, W. R. D., *Psychoanalytic Sudies of The Personality*, RKP,
1993

Foulkes, S. H., *Group Analytic Psychotherapy*, Maresfield, 1986

Freud, S., *Art and Literature*, Penguin, 1990

Freud, S., *The Psychopathology of Everyday Life*, Penguin, 1975

Freud, S., *The Essentials of Psychoanalysis, The Definitive Collection of Sigmund Freud's Writing*, Penguin, 1986

Fuller, M., *Atoms and Icons*, Mowbray, 1995

Graves, R. G., *The Greek Myths*, Penguin, 1960

Greenacre, P., *Trauma, Growth & Personality*, Maresfield, 1987

Hopkins, G. M., *The Major Poems*, Dent, 1979

Jansson, T., *Comet in Moominland*, Penguin, 1959

Jansson, T., *The Summer Book*, Penguin, 1977

Julian of Norwich, *Revelations of Divine Love*, Penguin, 1980

Jung, C. G., *Memories, Dreams, Reflections*, Fontana, 1983

Klein, J., *Our Need of Others and Its Roots in Infancy*, Routledge, 1987

Kovel, J., *A Complete Guide to Therapy*, Penguin, 1991

Lewis, C. S., *Surprised by Joy*, Fontana, 1976

Malan, D. H., *Individual Psychotherapy and the Science of Psychodynamics*, Butterworths, 1986

Mason, J., *Against Therapy*, Fontana, 1990

Miller, A., *The Drama of Being a Child*, Virago, 1987

Orwell, G., *Collected Essays*, Secker & Warburg, 1975

Ransom, A., *Peter Duck*, Penguin, 1968

Rushdie, S., *Midnight's Children*, Picador, 1982

Saint-Expeury, Antoine de, *The Little Prince*, Heinemann, 1945

Saint-Expeury, Antoine de, *Night Flight*, Penguin, 1976

Saint Augustine, *Confessions*, Penguin Classics, 1961

Shackleton, Sir Ernest, *South*, Heinemann, 1920

Singer, D. G. and J.L., *The House of Make-Believe*, Harvard, 1990

Sitwell, E., *English Eccentrics*, Penguin, 1973

Storr, A., *The Dynamics of Creation*, Penguin, 1991

136 Symington, N., *Narcissism, a New Theory*, Karnac Books, 1993

Symington, N., *The Analytic Experience*, Free Association Books, 1986

Symington, N., *Emotion and Spirit*, Cassell, 1994

Thompson, H. S., *The Great Shark Hunt*, Picador, 1979

Warner M., *From the Beast to the Blonde*, Chatto & Windus, 1994

Winnicott, D. W., *The Child, The Family and The Outside World*, Penguin, 1991

Winnicott, D. W., *Playing and Reality*, Penguin, 1990

Zipes, J., *Spells of Enchantment*, Viking, 1991